THE BATTLE FOR BIBLICAL BAPTISM

AN EXEGESIS OF SPIRIT AND WATER BAPTISM

BY
Luis C. Ruiz, Ph.D.

ISBN 978-1-7347481-7-8

All Scripture quotes are from the King James Bible except those verses compared and then the source is identified.

Address All Inquiries To:

THE OLD PATHS PUBLICATIONS, Inc.
142 Gold Flume Way
Cleveland, Georgia, U.S.A. 30528
Web: www.theoldpathspublications.com
E-mail: TOP@theoldpathspublications.com

DEDICATION

Every single thing we do in this life is possible because God gives us the ability. Whether we see, read, write or think only comes because of God's grace. In this manner, God uses us even though we are deeply flawed. It is Him that I must first thank. Along these lines, God also blessed me with a family without which I know this work would never have been possible. They often act as a mirror uncovering what I might have never noticed alone. I want to thank my editors (Paul Baran, Josh Bakr and my wife, Delia) who spent many hours providing me with valuable insight (and corrections). I also want to thank Dr. & Mrs. Williams for their ministry and love of the brethren. Last, I want to thank the many saints and local churches that have prayed and supported us over the last 20+ years. Our Lord Jesus used them in ways they may never realize.

Luis C. Ruiz, Ph.D.
May, 2020

Dear Richard
Thank you for your friendship in Christ for these many years. May the Lord Jesus continue to bless you & Cheryl and the rest of your family.

Luis

3

TABLE OF CONTENTS

TABLE OF CONTENTS

CHAPTER ONE – WORSHIP IN TRUTH

"To please God we must obey him. To obey God we must properly worship Him. To properly worship God we must properly interpret His precious Words. To properly interpret His Words we must submit to Him and His Spirit of Truth. And to submit to God we must rid ourselves of us." (Dr. Luis C. Ruiz)

In His infinite goodness, God has given the Church many spiritual gifts and blessings. If submitted to correctly and wisely, these gifts allow souls within the body of Christ to grow into maturity all the while bringing glory to the Creator of life. This fact encapsulates every aspect of the Christian's walk with God as they grow in grace and in the knowledge of Jesus Christ.

While the above truth may appear to be a relatively simple proposition to remember, it is often difficult to implement and even more difficult to maintain. When this ensues, believers will inevitably not grow in the Lord and not truly glorify God. Why? Because they are not worshipping Him in the true Spirit and in the Biblical truth as spoken by the Lord Jesus to the Samaritan woman at Jacob's well.

But the hour cometh, and now is, when the true worshippers shall worship the Father in spirit and in truth: for the Father seeketh such to worship him. God is a Spirit: and they that worship him must worship him in spirit and in truth. **(John 4:23-24)**

Sadly, there are many born-again believers, along with those who profess themselves as Christians, which are not worshipping God in Spirit and in truth. Stated oppositely, it literally means that they are worshipping God in a false or untruthful manner. It also means that they are worshipping God with their soul (emotions, intellect or experience) and not from their born-again spirit. This false worship can only stem from incorrectly applying or willfully ignoring the plain, common-sense, contextual, literal, grammatical method of interpretation used by Jesus and His Apostles. This is not a new phenomenon, as throughout the almost 2000 year history of the church every area of worship from giving, pastoral qualifications, the assembly of believers, the Lord's Supper etc. has been under spiritual attack. Over time every one of these areas of worship was mistakenly understood and eventually falsely practiced.

Baptism Under Attack

One area of worship that has been under perpetual spiritual attack since the early church is that of God-ordained baptism...more specifically the "doctrine of baptisms". This assault isn't surprising since water baptism has been practiced first within Biblical Judaism as demonstrated by the ministry of John the Baptist and second, practiced within the church body since Pentecost. Merge Spirit baptism into the doctrinal equation and it becomes evident how truth gets muddied and confusion reigns. The result being that the church body gets splintered while individual believers in Jesus Christ do not grow toward maturity.

It must be noted that this book is not an all-encompassing treatise on every single minor nuance pertaining to Biblical baptisms. However, this study will provide a detailed and comprehensive account of both water and Spirit baptism in their proper literary context. The book will also present the reader with clear exposition in order to rightly identify which type of baptism is being addressed.

This work also endeavors to breakdown the major fundamental elements of this very critical and essential issue in a Christian's walk with God. I specifically say 'essential' because there are some teachers and scholars that will carelessly say that knowledge and correct practice of the baptisms are not essential in Christianity. Some will even recklessly state that baptismal truths are not important...that they are tertiary at best. These "teachers" are undeniably saying that there are no truths associated with Biblical baptism...in effect injecting relativistic humanism into God's eternal veracities.

One other point about essentials versus non-essentials: while the proper knowledge and practice of the doctrine of baptisms may most times not be essential for eternal salvation, it is 100% unequivocally essential for growth in Christ; essential for progressive sanctification. When one reads God's inspired and preserved Scriptures, it becomes starkly apparent that almost all of it is not required for salvation (faith in Christ) but rather fully required (essential) for maturity in the Lord Jesus. Hence, if you adopt the "non-essential" mantra of some mainstream evangelical voices, then you would have to disregard 99% of the Bible as not having vitally important truths to embrace for godly living.

At this point, it would also be worthy to acknowledge that the understanding and teaching of Biblical baptism initially appears to be simple and mostly straightforward. However, when one begins to truly study the Scriptures, one quickly realizes the depth of the content. And as in all the major teachings of God, this results in much confusion about what the Bible actually says and commands about baptism.

This chaotic and divided approach toward baptisms in the body of Christ also comes through pride...the arrogance of man. This pride, in league with the wiles of Satan, creates a tempest that disorients many believers. In Luke 11:17, our Lord Jesus addresses this point in a slightly different context:

> *Every kingdom divided against itself is brought to desolation; and a house divided against a house falleth.*

Where there is confusion, there is division; this is what we see throughout the church, universally and locally. Thus, once a house (the church) is divided against itself, it begins to implode and eventually loses its ability to impart salt and light.

The Original Languages

This lovely doctrine of baptisms is one we can comprehend more fully when we begin to unravel what the original inspired languages state. In this case, we look at the language of the New Testament...Greek. Phonetically pronounced, here we find the Greek nouns "baptismos", "baptisma" and "baptistace" along with the Greek verbs "baptidzo" and "bapto". A simple reading of these Greek words clearly indicate that they were transliterated (not translated) into English words such as baptism and baptize. If these words would have been translated instead of transliterated into English the translation would almost unanimously be to immerse or sink.

The one instance where with the verb "baptidzo" does not mean immersion is noted in Luke 11:38.

And when the Pharisee saw it, he marvelled that he had not first washed before dinner.

Here the context clearly depicts that "baptidzo" is used to indicate our Master had not "washed" or bathed Himself before dinner. Other Greek verbs (such as "niptō" and "louō") are commonly translated into "wash". Hence, like in all other Biblical words, the context will drive the true meaning. (This treatise will later illustrate how the context will repeatedly drive the correct sense.)

Surprisingly, baptism (water or spiritual) is never mentioned in the Old Testament. We are only presented vague pictures or allusions of it in prior covenants or dispensations. Many have described the Israelite crossing of the Jordan River as being typological of New Testament baptism. In contrast, the worldwide flood of Noah and the Red Sea crossing are presented as reverse typologies. The Mosaic Law also outlines the washing of individuals, foods and other items again presenting vague allusions to the doctrine of baptisms.

Most Biblically-based scholars correctly describe baptism as a public demonstration that is exclusive to both the preparation for entering into the church age and for this age. (This will be covered more extensively throughout the work.) Hence, along with the permanent indwelling of the Holy Spirit, the Lord's Supper, the

Rapture and other attributes, baptism is only for the church...the body of Christ. (These are just a few reasons why the church couldn't start with Abraham as reformed/covenant theologians postulate.) The Bible in several places calls these events mysteries since they were not clearly prophetically outlined in the Old Testament. Some of the verses indicating these mysteries are found in Romans 11:25; 16:25; 1 Corinthians 15:51; Ephesians 3:9; 5:32; Colossians 1:26-27. Essentially, anything in the Epistles not prophesied in the Old Testament is touted as a mystery.

The Lord's Water Baptism

Along the lines of immersion, it is often forgotten that our Lord Jesus was baptized aka immersed. Reading Matthew 3:13-16:

> *Then cometh Jesus from Galilee to Jordan unto John, to be baptized of him. (Matt 3:13) But John forbad him, saying, I have need to be baptized of thee, and comest thou to me? (Matt 3:14) And Jesus answering said unto him, Suffer it to be so now: for thus it becometh us to fulfil all righteousness. Then he suffered him. (Matt 3:15) And Jesus, when he was baptized, went up straightway out of the water: and, lo, the heavens were opened unto him, and he saw the Spirit of God descending like a dove, and lighting upon him: (Matt 3:16)*

Jesus Christ voluntarily baptized himself. Joseph and Mary did not take Him to be baptized as an infant...they only took him to dedicate and circumcise him. So Jesus participated in all three. However, Jesus, as a man

(Immanuel) submitted Himself to the Father in heaven. So if circumcision replaced baptism as a few propose, then why did Jesus get circumcised and later immersed? (This will also be addressed later.)

The passage also details that Christ allowed Himself to be submersed because the Bible specifies that Christ rose from the river waters. If it were only a little sprinkling of water on the head it does not make sense to go into the river. All John the Baptist needed to do was to bring a container of water and pour it over Jesus.

As we delve deeper into our study we find that nowhere in the Bible do we find someone who is water baptized that did not request it...say for example an infant. We also never find a single example of sprinkling. (Later in the work we will Biblically reveal how both are teachings of man not of God.)

Returning to the original language, the Greek verb for baptism ("baptidzo") literally means to immerse, to dunk or to submerge completely. Of the 126 times we find the word in the Bible, only on a couple of occasions does it mean to be washed. In those instances, we are clearly guided by the passage's context. This is important to know when one studies the doctrine of baptisms in the Bible.

The Doctrine of Baptisms

Building on this thought, Hebrews 6:2 speaks of the doctrine of baptisms (plural) clearly indicating that there is more than one type of baptism.

Of the doctrine of baptisms, and of laying on of hands, and of resurrection of the dead, and of eternal judgment. (Hebrews 6:2)

Looking at it from the highest macro level, there are two kinds of baptisms or immersions: spiritual and water. Much of the confusion and division in the body of Christ comes from people incorrectly interpreting if the Bible is describing spiritual baptism or water baptism.

The Sources of Heresy

This author, as a Bible teacher, evangelist and preacher, acknowledges that some passages in the Bible are very difficult to interpret. But like any doctrinal error, false teaching or heresy they typically emanate from one of several sources.

- Many believers and teachers lack of Bible knowledge because they have not diligently studied. Sadly, some have never read the whole Bible.

- Some believers and teachers are not submitted to the Holy Spirit to lead them into all truth.

- Some teachers may not be born-again. They are professors not possessors!

- Some pastors and teachers desire being liked versus possibly offending someone with a Scriptural truth. For many it is just easier to get along.

- Gain of money or as the Bible calls it "filthy lucre". They may say, "They are paying me so why rock-the-boat."

- Some are emissaries of Satan. 2 Corinthians 11:15 tells us that Satan's ministers can be transformed to look like ministers of righteousness whose purpose is to seek, kill and destroy.

In spite of these obstacles, which many of us have been exposed to, we will forge ahead and begin to scrutinize the inner working of the doctrine of baptisms.

Speaking specifically of spiritual baptism, we will study that there is only one for the believer and it occurs when a person trusts Jesus as God and Savior...when one is born again. There are several verses on this beautiful truth.

> *For John truly baptized with water; but ye shall be baptized with the Holy Ghost not many days hence.* *(Acts 1:5)*

Here as in Matthew 3:10 and Luke 3:16, we read of the still future arrival of what we know today as the baptism of the Holy Spirit. And to eliminate confusion, the Holy Spirit has always existed but had never before baptized a human...never made a permanent home next to the spirit of a person after faith.

In Acts 10, we read a passage that records what happened when the Apostle Peter preached to the first converted Gentiles. This passage clearly distinguishes spiritual baptism and water baptism.

> *While Peter yet spake these words, the Holy Ghost fell on all them which heard the word.* *(Acts 10:44)* *And they of the circumcision which believed were astonished, as many as came with Peter, because that on the Gentiles also was poured out the gift of the*

Holy Ghost. (Acts 10:45) For they heard them speak with tongues (literal languages with structure not gibberish), and magnify God. Then answered Peter, (Acts 10:46) Can any man forbid water, that these should not be baptized, which have received the Holy Ghost as well as we? (Acts 10:47) And he commanded them to be baptized in the name of the Lord. Then prayed they him to tarry certain days. (Acts 10:48) (emphasis added)

We read in verse 45 how the Holy Spirit baptized or fell on the Gentiles (not the Jews; not the Samaritans) and in verses 47-48, after receiving the gift of God's Spirit, the focus shifts to them being baptized by water. In this passage, God clearly contrasts what it is to receive the Spirit of God...to be spiritually baptized with the act of being baptized by water. They are two separate things: one is to enter the body of Christ...to be saved; the latter is about being obedient, offering a public testimony and receiving blessings. Later we'll spend time on developing that water baptism is an external/public depiction of what God has done on the inside.

A passage that gives us more clarity on this doctrine is found in 1 Corinthians 1:14-17.

I thank God that I baptized none of you, but Crispus and Gaius; (1Cor 1:14) Lest any should say that I had baptized in mine own name. (1Cor 1:15) And I baptized also the household of Stephanas: besides, I know not whether I baptized any other. (1Cor 1:16) For Christ sent me not to baptize, but to preach the gospel: not with wisdom of words, lest the cross of Christ should be made of none effect. **(1Cor 1:17)**

Christ did not send Paul to baptize by water but to preach the Gospel of eternal salvation through faith in Jesus Christ. For the Apostle Paul, it was weightier to bring souls to Christ. If water baptism were essential for salvation (or to be part of the Bride of Christ) then he would have done it. But since water baptism was not a requirement to go to heaven or be Christ's Bride, the Holy Spirit through the Apostle Paul did not prioritize it.

Essential for Growth

On the other hand, although it isn't necessary to be baptized by water to go to heaven, God provides us with many clear Scriptural examples and directives so that we could follow them. These Biblical examples are given for our sake...in order to bless us. So while water baptism is not essential for salvation it is essential for growth. We'll address this topic later in the book.

In addition, some mistakenly teach that a Christian can receive the baptism of the Holy Spirit post-salvation. And although there are some hard-to-understand passages (which we'll cover extensively), one of the principles of Bible interpretation is that one establishes doctrine on clear and easy-to-understand references. One uses the more understandable verses/passages to understand the more difficult ones. Using this principle we turn to 1 Corinthians 12:12-13:

For as the body is one, and hath many members, and all the members of that one body, being many, are one body: so also is Christ. For by one Spirit are we all baptized into one body, whether we be Jews or Gentiles, whether we be bond or free; and have been all made to drink into one Spirit.

Verse 12 states that all that are born again, regenerated, saved are of the same body...the metaphorical body of Christ. In verse 13, we read that **all** who are in the body of Christ were baptized into one body. Whether Jewish or Gentile, **all** who have believed that Jesus is God and Savior have received the same Holy Spirit. This clearly says that all Christians are baptized in the Holy Spirit. There is no-one that is saved...that is going to heaven that does not have the baptism/indwelling of the Holy Spirit of God. This is further established by Ephesians 4:5-6

One Lord, one faith, one baptism, One God and Father of all, who is above all, and through all, and in you all.

There is only one Lord, one faith and one spiritual baptism into the body of Christ. As the Bible says, that baptism occurs when we are justified and adopted by God. This happens at the beginning of our journey with God...when we first become born again.

In summarizing this initial chapter, let's outline some of its more significant points.

- The baptism of the Holy Spirit occurs when one accepts Jesus as God and Savior. (This is fully covered in chapters five through eight.)

- Spirit baptism gives you entrance to the body of Christ.

- A false gospel says that one needs to be baptized by water to go to heaven. (This is fully covered in chapter eleven.)

- In this church age, there is no second work of the Holy Spirit or a spiritual baptism that occurs after salvation. The instances where this took place was when the Holy Spirit was being introduced during the establishment of the Church. (This is fully covered in chapters five through eight.)

- What happens after the initial Holy Spirit baptism is described in the Bible as "being filled by the Spirit". (This is covered in chapter nine.)

Doctrinal yet Devotional

In concluding this first chapter, a couple of points should be addressed. While this treatise is largely doctrinal, as described earlier, it greatly overlaps with how one obeys and worships our Mighty God. In this way, the book becomes a devotional and guide to some areas of Christian living.

Additionally, this book is meant to assist believers that are struggling to comprehend what occurs at the moment of salvation and what happens later in our journey with God. Many are in bondage because they have been instructed to seek eternal salvation in one of two ways: First, via an emotional experience through a so-called second blessing; second, via the work of water baptism. Tragically, these views make a mockery of Ephesians 2:8-9.

> *For by grace are ye saved through faith; and that not of yourselves: it is the gift of*

God: Not of works, lest any man should boast.

Many well-intended souls have simply not been taught the simplicity of receiving the gift of salvation by faith in the Deity and work of Jesus Christ. Once you trust in Jesus Christ as Saviour and God you are indwelled (baptized) by the Holy Spirit and given God's power to truly overcome your struggles and uncertainties. It is after you are given this supernatural strength that you can start trusting Him in other areas of your life and can start doing works for Him. This is an amazing promise offered first to whosoever believes and afterwards to whosoever submits.

When we are assured of how to receive eternal salvation and what is subsequently needed to grow in Christ's grace then we can follow and obey His decrees. The outcome of trusting these truths allow us to better rest in Jesus' gentle yoke. It is only then that we can have a more abundant, more joyful life. This is what we should all desire. Amen!

CHAPTER TWO – BAPTIZE IN THE HOLY GHOST & BAPTIZE WITH FIRE

"Study the Bible to discover how to prove!"
(Dr. Luis C. Ruiz)

Let's start this chapter with a bit baptismal humor.

> *Johnny's Mother looked out the window and noticed Him "playing church" with their cat. He had the cat sitting quietly and he was preaching to it. She smiled and went about her work.*
>
> *A while later she heard loud meowing and hissing. She ran back to the open window to see Johnny baptizing the cat in a tub of water.*
>
> *She called out, "Johnny, stop that! The cat is afraid of water!" Johnny looked up at her and said, "He should have thought about that before he joined my church!"*

Prior to developing our next topic it would be beneficial to review a couple of pertinent Scriptures. We established, through Hebrews 6:2 that there is more than one kind of baptism during the church age.

> *Of the doctrine of baptisms, and of laying on of hands, and of resurrection of the dead, and of eternal judgment.*

We also studied that baptisms can be divided into two categories: spiritual baptism and water baptism. We further established that a believer's spiritual baptism occurs when a soul believes in Jesus as God and Messiah. It is at this precise point-in-time that the soul is placed into the body of Christ...the Church of God. Two verses justify this truth: 1 Corinthians 12:13 and Ephesians 4:5.

> *For by one Spirit are we all baptized into one body, whether we be Jews or Gentiles, whether we be bond or free; and have been all made to drink into one Spirit.*

> *One Lord, one faith, one baptism.*

Spiritual Baptism by Fire

Building on these verses let's examine another way that spiritual baptism is depicted in Scripture. In the Gospels of Matthew and Luke we are told by John the Baptist that there is a Baptism by the Holy Ghost as well as a Baptism by fire. In order to study Baptism by Fire let's turn to Matthew 3:5-13. (See also Luke 3:16-17 for a parallel reading.)

> *Then went out to him Jerusalem, and all Judaea, and all the region round about Jordan, (Matt 3:5) And were baptized of him in Jordan, confessing their sins. (Matt 3:6) But when he saw many of the Pharisees and Sadducees come to his baptism, he said unto them, O generation of vipers, who hath warned you to flee from the wrath to come? (Matt 3:7) Bring forth therefore fruits meet for repentance: (Matt 3:8) And think not to say within yourselves, We have Abraham to our father: for I say unto you, that God is able of these stones to raise up children unto Abraham. (Matt 3:9) And now also the*

axe is laid unto the root of the trees: therefore every tree which bringeth not forth good fruit is hewn down, and cast into the fire. (Matt 3:10) I indeed baptize you with water unto repentance: but he that cometh after me is mightier than I, whose shoes I am not worthy to bear: he shall baptize you with the Holy Ghost, and with fire: (Matt 3:11) Whose fan is in his hand, and he will throughly purge his floor, and gather his wheat into the garner; but he will burn up the chaff with unquenchable fire. (Matt 3:12) Then cometh Jesus from Galilee to Jordan unto John, to be baptized of him. (Matt 3:13)

Beginning in verse 5, the Bible tells us that John the Baptist was baptizing in the Jordan River all who wanted to confess and repent of their sins. The repentant came from all parts of Judea to make this public act of worship. (What is called "the Baptism of John" will be addressed in chapter four.)

In verse 7, John the Baptist saw that the Pharisees and Sadducees came to watch but not participate in either baptism or repentance. It is noteworthy that although the Pharisees and the Sadducees did not get along for several reasons, they formed a league against their common enemy, John the Baptist. (They later linked once more to become common adversaries of our Lord Jesus Christ.)

In verse 7, John begins a discourse that lasts six verses. First, he calls the Pharisees and Sadducees vipers (Vipers are not only snakes but venomous ones.) He then asks them a question:

...who hath warned you to flee from the wrath to come?

This question was asked by the Baptist because it was largely evident that these unconverted religious leaders did not know how to escape the wrath of God. John immediately gives them the answer:

Bring forth therefore fruits meet for repentance.

As we read, many were there repenting and being baptized but not the Pharisees and Sadducees.

The Jewish Leaders versus John the Baptist

The Holy Spirit, through John the Baptist, addressed the Jewish leaders this way because He knew their prideful heart; that they believed that entry to heaven was earned merely because they were descendants of Abraham. (This is similar to many today thinking that they will enter Heaven because they are a member of a church, sect or family.)

How misguided they were/are because when God chooses people (like He elected the Jews), He chooses to serve a purpose...for service. So while the Jews were elected that was still not sufficient to get them into heaven because the Bible gives us many examples of unregenerate Jews. Remember that God is able to choose stones to serve His purposes.

Paraphrasing verses 9 and 10: "Do not presume that you are going to heaven not having a relationship with the true God because the axe is ready to cut trees (souls) who do not give good fruit." And not only will they be cut off but they also will be cast into the fire. This means the following: a person who does not have saving faith in God is not going to be able to demonstrate good fruit. And since they cannot demonstrate good fruit they will be cast into the fire. John the Baptist is talking about judgment, condemnation. That is the context.

In verse 11, John tells us that he only baptized with water for repentance, but that Jesus the Messiah will come to baptize in two ways: with the Holy Spirit and with fire. And it is here that several have poorly and inexplicably interpreted that these two baptisms are blessings to be sought.

In verse 12, John tells us that Christ with his fan or winnower will separate the good grain...the wheat (which is useful) from the straw (which is not useful). And after the Lord Jesus separates it, He will pick up the good grain for Himself and will burn the straw into the fire that never dies...the unquenchable fire.

Baptized by Flames

By the context of the full passage, it is clear that it is describing the damnation of souls in hell for eternity; a condemnation where souls will consciously suffer in perpetuity. The straw is a metaphor of a soul that will be baptized by fire....immersed, surrounded by flames.

Sadly, there are some in the charismatic movement who believe that Baptism by Fire and Baptism by the Holy Ghost are essentially the same and hence are something positive...something that everyone in the body of Christ should earnestly desire. This happens largely because it is often related with another doctrine...what is called the second work or baptism of the Holy Spirit. (This will be covered later in the book.) Even worse, there are teachers/pastors who incredibly teach that the Holy Spirit will baptize certain believers in fire…which is an abominable teaching. Heartbreakingly, there are many who blindly follow this false teaching and ask God to baptize them by fire; never carefully reading the Word in order to truly understand what God intends for their life.

The Wheat and the Tares

Another passage that offers a similar teaching is found in Matthew 13:24-30.

Another parable put he forth unto them, saying,

The kingdom of heaven is likened unto a man which sowed good seed in his field: **(Matt 13:24)** *But while men slept, his enemy came and sowed tares among the wheat, and went his way.* **(Matt 13:25)** *But when the blade was sprung up, and brought forth fruit, then appeared the tares also.* **(Matt 13:26)** *So the servants of the householder came and said unto him, Sir, didst not thou sow good seed in thy field? from whence then hath it tares?* **(Matt 13:27)** *He said unto them, An enemy hath done this. The servants said unto him, Wilt thou then that we go and gather them up?* **(Matt 13:28)** *But he said, Nay; lest while ye gather up the tares, ye root up also the wheat with them.* **(Matt 13:29)** *Let both grow together until the harvest: and in the time of harvest I will say to the reapers, Gather ye together first the tares, and bind them in bundles to burn*

them: but gather the wheat into my barn.
(Matt 13:30)

The full explanation for this passage is found in Matthew 13:36-43, but let me provide a brief overview that supports this chapter's context.

The man (representative of Jesus Christ) sowed good seed (representative of the sons or servants of the Kingdom of God) in the field (which is representative of the world). When the servants of the Lord were sleeping i.e. not watching the enemy (representative of the devil), tares were sown (representative of the sons of the Devil).

In verse 27, the children of the kingdom blamed their Lord for the multitude of evil people in the world and the pervasive sin therein. Sadly, they neglected that part of the reason there was so much evil in the world was because they themselves were not obeying, not working, not being vigilant.

Then the tenor changes; in verse 28 just after being convinced of their sin and error, they overreact (a typical response). In this case, the overreaction was to uproot and gather the tares...the children of the devil. The counsel of Christ then states that they shouldn't pluck out anything from the field because they could damage or hurt the good, the wheat...the true believer.

The advice from the man (Jesus Christ) was to just let the tares grow in their midst for now. Hence, if someone declares belief in Jesus Christ, we should never judge whether they are saved or not. We can judge their actions and sins against God but not their standing with God.

Following, the Lord said that He will send harvesting angels to collect the weeds (the children of the Devil) during the harvest or end of the world. These angels will take the tares/weeds (the children of the Devil) into the furnace of fire where there will be weeping and gnashing of teeth.

The angels will also pick up the wheat (the good, the just) and place them in the barn of the Lord (Heaven) so that the Lord can make more use of them. In the end, we are told that the righteous (wheat) will shine like the sun in the Kingdom of their Father.

Here it is clear to understand that the wheat is good because it is useful and that the tares are not useful and are burned in the fire. Thus, connecting it with our study, God does not want anyone to be baptized by fire but wants all to get baptized into His family as an adopted son or daughter.

Contextual Confusion

Perhaps some of the confusion around "Baptism by Fire" arises because the word fire, depending on the context, can mean several things. In these few other anomalies, fire can mean: purification of works (1 Corinthians 3:12-15; Revelation 3:18), difficult tests for the believer (1 Peter 1:7) and the word of God that spread like a fire at Pentecost (Acts 2). However, in almost all of the 79 verses where we see the word "fire" used in the New Testament, the context means judgment and what happens after the judgment. This is what is clearly read in the case of "Baptism by "Fire".

Regarding context and interpretation here is a good quote to remember:

"We should read the entire Bible and note the context before launching with an opinion that can wreck the faith of another soul."

So it should be very clear that this "baptism by fire" is something that a soul should never want. What a soul should do/want: is to self-examine to determine if they are truly in the faith...if they truly have the Holy Spirit dwelling inside of them. In other words, if they have been baptized in the Holy Spirit at conversion; by believing that Jesus Christ is God, and died and resurrected for them.

After that, a believer should desire to learn what God requires of them by reading the Bible and being in prayer with God. They should long to obey God. This obedience, if it comes from God, should desire to be baptized in water via immersion.

As stated earlier, God's will is for all true professing believers to be water baptized publicly. Once we submit in obedience, God will shower us with favor even more abundantly. Alleluia!

CHAPTER THREE – WATER BAPTISM

"Many under the title of Christian have become modern day Pontius Pilates regarding Truth. Heaven, hell, salvation, creation, the second coming, miracles are just stories to be manipulated and changed at the whim of man and so-called tradition."
(Dr. Luis C. Ruiz)

Before embarking on the topic of Water Baptism let's do a brief review. First, we established that there is one spiritual baptism that occurs for all who freely accept the gift and believe in Jesus as Messiah/God. Their spirit is then baptized into the body of Christ.

We also studied that spiritual baptism by fire is a condemnation and occurs when a soul rejects Jesus as Savior. Recall the parable that wheat (representative of believers) is collected to live with Christ for eternity while tares or weeds (those that are lost without Christ) are thrown into the fire that will never be quenched. In this context the fire refers to hell and eventually the Lake of fire.

Doctrinal Importance

Regarding the subject of water baptism, similar to most doctrinal issues, it is an extremely important subject to comprehend. This is why Satan has attacked this critical doctrine causing much division within the church. Much, if not all, of this division has been caused by the pride and the self-righteousness of man. As such, there are five major errors or heresies regarding baptism by water.

The first error says that infants can be baptized. This heresy gives many who have been baptized as infants a false sense of security in Christ. Sadly, some will even postulate that infants have "unconscious faith" that can either be standalone or part of the parent's faith. These grave errors will be summarily refuted using Scriptures themselves.

The second error states that baptism does not mean immersion in water but rather sprinkling or christening. We have already discussed the baptism of our Lord Jesus but will also provide other verses to refute this false teaching. We must never forget that God's edicts have always been exact; altering them even in the smallest way is disobedience.

The third error says one needs to be baptized by water to go to heaven. This is very serious and can be considered a damnable heresy (2 Peter 2:1) because it links salvation to a type of work. In truth, this teaching generates an additional stumbling block to those that are truly seeking God!

The fourth error says that the baptism by water is not important, non-essential or possibly not for the church age. While this heresy does not impact a soul's eternal destination it will undoubtedly impact a soul's Christian walk and their ability to abide in Christ.

The fifth and final error states that you have to be a mature and learned Christian before being baptized. This heresy creates unbiblical hurdles that can deter or prevent a believer from being Biblically immersed through obedience.

Biblical Evidence

So let's traverse the Bible in order to understand what Biblical water baptism is while at the same time refuting these five grave errors. For this endeavor, we turn to God's Words to the Acts of the Apostles 8:26.

> *And the angel of the Lord spake unto Philip, saying, Arise, and go toward the south unto the way that goeth down from Jerusalem unto Gaza, which is desert.*

This verse speaks of Philip the deacon not the Apostle because the Apostles for now remained in Jerusalem (Acts 8:1). Moving to verse 27:

> *And he arose and went: and, behold, a man of Ethiopia, an eunuch of great authority under Candace queen of the Ethiopians, who had the charge of all her treasure, and had come to Jerusalem for to worship, (Acts 8:27) Was returning, and sitting in his chariot read Esaias the prophet. (Acts 8:28)*

The eunuch was a Jewish man (or proselyte) of great authority living in Ethiopia. He was returning to Ethiopia after the conclusion of the Jewish holy days in Jerusalem and was reading from the prophet Isaiah. Moving to verse 29:

> *Then the Spirit said unto Philip, Go near, and join thyself to this chariot. (Acts 8:29) And Philip ran thither to him, and heard him read the prophet Esaias, and said, Understandest thou what thou readest? (Acts 8:30)*

Philip was in complete submission to the direction of the Holy Spirit so much so that he didn't take his time walking to the chariot but rather he ran to it. He didn't hesitate one moment. He didn't say:

"Well Lord, I'm not sure if I should go to this man. You know he seems to be kind of important. He is also really wrapped up in reading something. I probably shouldn't interrupt him. Besides, the chariot will be gone in another 10 seconds so why bother."

Philip urgently hurries toward the chariot and because of his immediate obedience; he overhears the Eunuch struggling with a prophetic text. Just from hearing the eunuch's laboring with Scripture, Philip asks a simple but yet profound question:

"Do you understand what you are reading?"

This verse speaks to the need for good, solid Bible teaching since many (like the Ethiopian Eunuch) do not understand what they are reading. Like Philip, all qualified Bible teachers should sincerely ask questions in a loving manner. The Eunuch, in humility, responds in verse 31:

...How can I, except some man should guide me? And he desired Philip that he would come up and sit with him.

Although he was Jewish and was evidently fulfilling his tri-annual obligatory pilgrimage to the Jerusalem feasts, the eunuch still did not understand what he was reading. Wanting to learn, he admitted his ignorance...his lack of knowledge. Not only did he profess his ignorance but also asked for guidance and eventually invited Philip up into the chariot. (As an aside, all of us should set aside our pride and earnestly ask others to help us gain deeper understanding of God's life giving words.) Moving to verses 32 through 35:

> The place of the scripture which he read was this,

> *He was led as a sheep to the slaughter; and like a lamb dumb before his shearer, so opened he not his mouth: (Acts 8:32) In his humiliation his judgment was taken away: and who shall declare his generation? for his life is taken from the earth. (Acts 8:33) And the eunuch answered Philip, and said, I pray thee, of whom speaketh the prophet this? of himself, or of some other man? (Acts 8:34) Then Philip opened his mouth, and began at the same scripture, and preached unto him Jesus. (Acts 8:35)*

From Isaiah 53:7-8, Philip interpreted the messianic prophecy that was fulfilled by Jesus and preached the Messiah's message of eternal salvation.

Jesus Affirms Isaiah

As a side note, some false teachers (albeit with PhDs) teach that Isaiah did not write Isaiah chapters 40 through 66. (They will state that this section was written much later and call this so-called other writer "Deutero-Isaiah".) Yet in verse 28 as well as in other places in the New Testament we have a direct refutation of this false teaching. So if someone believed that Isaiah didn't write chapter 53 then you would have to also deny this and other passages. Hence, another proof of the Bible's integrated, foolproof, miraculous design! Turning to verse 36 and 37:

And as they went on their way, they came unto a certain water: and the eunuch said, See, here is water; what doth hinder me to be baptized? **(Acts 8:36)** *And Philip said, If thou believest with all thine heart, thou mayest. And he answered and said, I believe that Jesus Christ is the Son of God.* **(Acts 8:37)**

The eunuch now asks Philip a key question: *"What prevents me from being baptized?"* Philip assuredly answered him: *"if you believe with all your heart that Jesus Christ is the Son of God"*...then nothing prevents you. (Recall that Philip had explained to him that Jesus was the one sacrificed and that He was an offering to man's sin as prophesied in Isaiah 53.) We're then told that the eunuch believed in his heart and then professed *"Yes, I believe that Jesus Christ is the Son of God"*.

Here is confirmation that the act of being water baptized comes after a soul professes Jesus as Savior. All verses where someone is water baptized portray a person that believes Jesus is God. This is very clear. Never does a verse refer to an infant without knowledge. While some verses speak of all the members of a house being baptized (Acts 16:15; 18:8) never is a baby mentioned. You must inject theological bias in order to extract and believe that an infant is baptized in the passages.

Believe then Be Baptized

Earlier in the chapter God provides another verse that mentions one must believe before being water baptized. Speaking of the same Philip in Acts 8:12:

> *But when they believed Philip preaching the things concerning the kingdom of God, and the name of Jesus Christ, they were baptized, both men and women.*

Again men and women...no small children and certainly no infants!

Likewise, Joseph and Mary did not baptize baby Jesus but solely circumcised and dedicated him in the temple. (Both acts were Jewish Mosaic Law statutes that do not apply to the church.) Instead, we read that Jesus, of his own will, in obedience to the Father, was baptized at about the age of 30. Reformed theology would have you believe that infant baptism replaced circumcision. However, no Biblical evidence for this exists...just Scripture twisting and "proof-texting" that will be addressed later in the treatise.

Returning to Acts 8:38-39 with Philip and the Eunuch:

> *And he commanded the chariot to stand still: and they went down both into the water, both Philip and the eunuch; and he baptized him. And when they were come up out of the water, the Spirit of the Lord caught away Philip, that the eunuch saw him no more: and he went on his way rejoicing.*

Both Philip and the Eunuch dismounted the chariot, went down into the water and came up from the water. This clearly indicates that water baptism is via immersion, entering fully into the water. This is literally what the Greek verb "baptidzo" means and is the same verb used for the baptism of our Lord Jesus.

Complete Immersion

If immersion wasn't a requirement, Philip would have just brought a cup of water from the River and poured it over the Eunuch's head. Similarly, John the Baptist would have walked around with jugs or wet cloths to sprinkle on foreheads. Likewise, Jesus would not have gone into the Jordan but would have called John to come out of the river. It can't be much clearer than this.

Briefly addressing church history, the exclusive practice of the early church was water baptism via immersion. You will find many ancient churches that built spacious pools to immerse, often in large groups. Many writings of the 2nd and 3rd century confirm these large pools and the adherence to Biblical baptism. As the church became more corrupted with Romanist observances, infant baptism started to be practiced. This resulted in the pools being covered and subsequently replaced by sprinkling fountains.

There are many reasons why infant baptism started to infiltrate the church. Through false teaching, parents of newborns feared for the eternal damnation of the baby's soul if he were to die. Thus, they began to sprinkle them in the false hope of giving them eternal life in Christ. This deceitful teaching also insured that people would register the babies for "christening" which allowed the church and government to keep a census for people control and tax revenue purposes. Another reason was that it became a money-making service offering for these false teachers.

While the dark ages permeated much of Christendom, by God's grace there were still faithful

Christian groups like the Albigenses and the Waldensians that observed Biblical believer's baptism. As the dark ages waned, many of the Protestant Reformers (who were themselves Roman Catholic) protested and rejected Romanist salvation by works but unfortunately kept errant teachings like infant baptism and replacement theology.

Spiritually Dangerous Teachings

Other spiritually dangerous teachings surrounding water baptism include:

- You must be a member of a church for a period of time in order to get baptized.
- You must eliminate certain sins or grow more in Christ before being baptized.
- You can only be baptized in the name of Jesus. (This heresy will be focused on in chapter ten.)

These teachings are man-made and nowhere to be found in the Bible. The simple truth is that you only need to believe in Christ as your Saviour in order to get immersed in water. Passage upon passage illustrates this wonderful truth. Scripturally, you can get "dunked" the very same day you believe in Jesus Christ as Saviour.

Another water baptismal falsehood is the one that states that you must be baptized by water to go to heaven. (This will be covered more fully in chapter eleven) This is very serious as it disregards the many passages that separate saving faith and water baptism. An often misused verse is Mark 16:16 which states:

He that believeth and is baptized shall be saved; but he that believeth not shall be damned.

It is here that some confuse baptism of the Holy Spirit (which indeed does occur at salvation) with baptism by water. But if you read the second half of the verse - it is clear that not being baptized by water will not condemn you.

...but he that believeth not shall be damned.

In addition, let's not forget what our Lord told the penitent criminal who was crucified next to Him in Luke 23:43:

Verily I say unto thee, To day shalt thou be with me in paradise.

Here, the forgiven sinner did not have the opportunity to be baptized by water but yet was with Jesus that very day! Why? Because he believed in Jesus as Savior when he said to him in the previous verse:

Lord, remember me when you come into your Kingdom.

By his faith the crucified sinner was eternally pardoned, and went with Christ initially to paradise and eventually to the third heaven. He did not need to be baptized by water.

Why Get Immersed?

The last false teaching that we will examine in this section is one that states that since it isn't necessary to be baptized by water to go to heaven then why should I do it? In this scenario, we should remember this uncomplicated truth: there is only one thing a soul needs to be saved and that is to believe in Christ as God and Savior. Hence, everything else that God commands us to do (including water baptism) is necessary in order to live in God's perfect will, necessary to receive blessings here on Earth and necessary to receive heavenly crowns. Quite simply stated, living in Christ is to obey him. Thus, water baptism is simply an act of faith and obedience that publically identifies you with Christ the Lord.

If you believe and identify with Jesus Christ your next step of obedience is to be baptized by water if you have not done so. Don't allow excuses **or** pride **or** fear of water steal the blessings that God wants to give you as well as the blessing you can be for someone else.

> *And Jesus came and spake unto them, saying, All power is given unto me in heaven and in earth. (Matt 28:18) Go ye therefore, and teach all nations, baptizing them in the name of the Father, and of the Son, and of the Holy Ghost: (Matt 28:19) Teaching them to observe all things whatsoever I have commanded you: and, lo, I am with you alway, even unto the end of the world. Amen. (Matt 28:20)*

CHAPTER FOUR – JOHN THE BAPTIST'S BAPTISM OF REPENTANCE

"Every soul has some form of bias. If someone thinks they have no bias...that itself is biased. We must let God rid ourselves of it as much as is heavenly possible!" (Dr. Luis C. Ruiz)

Continuing our examination on the doctrine of baptisms we begin to look more closely at what the Bible calls "The Baptism of John". It is a very important topic and one that unfortunately is seldom studied. I truly believe if more churches studied this specific aspect more deeply, perhaps many of the divisions and misunderstandings about Spiritual and Water Baptism would be eradicated.

Apollos and Baptism

To start us off, we will examine a passage in the book of Acts chapter 19. Prior to reading the passage, let's summarize the latter portion of chapter 18 to develop the context. There we read of the eloquent and Biblically well-instructed travelling evangelist, Apollos. We're told that Apollos was fervent in spirit and boldly preached the Scriptures in the synagogues. Above all, what makes this account unique and distinctive is that Apollos was able to be "mighty" in the Old Testament Scriptures while only knowing/experiencing the Baptism of John. (This is key to understanding other accounts.)

We then read about how (in Ephesus) the faithful discipleship couple of Aquila and Priscilla more accurately explained the ways of God. (Earlier in Acts

18, we're told how they also discipled the Apostle Paul early in his ministry.) They explained to Apollos how Jesus satisfied the prophecies of Messiah while also providing him with deeper doctrinal understanding.

As Apollos travelled to Achaia (armed with the truth that the Messiah already came) his public evangelistic ministry became even more effective as he convinced many Jews (via Scripture) that Jesus was the Christ. Apollos was also now able to powerfully disciple those that had believed in Jesus Christ. Previously, solely operating under the Baptism of John, Apollos was limited in his understanding of Immanuel...God the Son.

Thus, after believing the progressive revelation beyond the "Baptism of John", Apollos had now taken his service for God to another level of faith and maturity. So much so that on other occasions as documented in 1 Corinthians and Titus he was compared to the Apostles Peter and Paul. This brings us to Acts chapter 19.

> And it came to pass, that, while Apollos was at Corinth, Paul having passed through the upper coasts came to Ephesus: and finding certain disciples, (Acts 19:1) He said unto them, Have ye received the Holy Ghost since ye believed? And they said unto him, We have not so much as heard whether there be any Holy Ghost. (Acts 19:2) And he said unto them, Unto what then were ye baptized? And they said, Unto John's baptism. (Acts 19:3) Then said Paul, John verily baptized with the baptism of repentance, saying unto the people, that they should believe on him which should

come after him, that is, on Christ Jesus. (Acts 19:4) When they heard this, they were baptized in the name of the Lord Jesus. (Acts 19:5) And when Paul had laid his hands upon them, the Holy Ghost came on them; and they spake with tongues, and prophesied. (Acts 19:6)

The Jews of Acts 19

Through the leading of the Holy Spirit, in vs. 2 Paul asks these disciples (they were clearly saved believers based on the context): *"Have ye received the Holy Ghost since ye believed?"* The reading of *"since ye believed"* would certainly indicate that the reception of the Holy Spirit took place subsequent to salvation. This was absolutely true in this situation and during the formative stages of the church. In view here is that believing Jews were transitioning from the Mosaic Law.

The disciples' response was that they hadn't even heard that God's Spirit would take an active part in their faith. Again, this would have been an absolutely correct statement given that the dispensation of the Law of Moses was now overlapping with the Grace or the Church Dispensation.

In verse 3, rather than calling into question their belief in Jesus, Paul then follows up with a logical second question, *"Unto what then were you baptized?"* Their answer—*"Unto John's baptism"*—shows why they had not yet received the Spirit; they had only submitted to John's baptism. With that response, the Apostle Paul knew where these disciples were spiritually and what needed to follow.

What is important about these disciples (similar to Apollos) is that by faith they had prepared themselves for the coming baptism of the Holy Spirit. In the next verse, Paul reaffirms them of the validity and importance of "John's Baptism" by stating that it focused on repentance...which in context is Jewish souls turning away from their sins and turning back to God.

Still Awaiting the Messiah

We must remember that never before had faith in God been accompanied by the indwelling and sealing work of the Holy Spirit. Here is the key: these Jewish believers were saved by faith through the revelation given by the Law of Moses and the prophets. Additionally, operating under John the Baptist's Baptism indicated that they were still awaiting the Messiah. As a result, they were not aware that several events had taken place. These events were:

- That Jesus the Christ (the Anointed One) was born of a virgin in Bethlehem.
- That Jesus the Christ came with mighty signs and wonders validating His Deity as Immanuel.
- That Jesus the Christ was crucified (During the Feast of Passover), buried three days (During the Feast of Unleavened Bread) and miraculously resurrected (During the Feast of First Fruits).
- That Jesus the Christ walked among many for 40 days post resurrecting after which He miraculously ascended into the clouds to be at the right-hand of the Father.
- That Jesus the Christ satisfied hundreds of Old Testament Messianic prophecies and that all of the writings of Moses and the prophets spoke of Him.

- That the Holy Spirit (the Comforter) came with mighty power during "Shavuot" (the Feast of Weeks or Pentecost).

Paul also added that part of John's baptism of repentance was to believe on the One coming after him…Christ Jesus. It's interesting how Paul differentiates between repentance and belief, rendering each distinguishable. Hence, repentance is not belief. So while repentance (change of mind) accompanies saving faith, repentance does not always lead to it.

The Apostle Paul likely explained everything that Jesus did; for example the fulfilling of hundreds of Old Testament prophecies, eventually being killed on the Passover. He likely told them how "Yehoshua" miraculously conquered death on the Feast of First Fruits and eventually ascended into the heavens after 40 days of life and miracles. He then no doubt described how the Holy Spirit followed seven days later with great power and signs. Hence, the isolated disciples hadn't vainly believed in John's baptism because we read how they immediately added to what they already knew to be true and were re-baptized in water in the name of the Lord Jesus.

This will be addressed later, but some (often called Oneness Pentecostals) have used Acts 19:5 (and other verses) as a primary reason to further divide the cause of Jesus Christ. As such, they baptize only in the name of the Lord Jesus, not in the name of the Father, Son and Holy Ghost while also believing it is a necessary work for salvation.

To Prepare Israel for the Messiah

Returning to the Baptism of John, it is critical to note that John the Baptist's ministry was aimed specifically at the nation of Israel in preparation for the potential establishment of their promised messianic kingdom.

> *When John had first preached before his coming the baptism of repentance to all the people of Israel.* **(Acts 13:24)**

Here we're clearly shown that John the Baptist's baptism of repentance was for the Jewish nation. In some circles, pastors/teachers incorrectly interpret "the people of Israel" and blur them with the church. They allegorize "people of Israel" without any Biblical license to do so. When this happens hundreds of passages in the Bible are distorted and confusing.

Another verse that provides us with an important clue is Matthew 11:13.

> *For all the prophets and the law prophesied until John.* (See also Luke 16:16)

In effect, John was the last Old Testament prophet. Some may say, "Wasn't John the Baptist in the Gospels and aren't the Gospels in the New Testament?" This is true from a man-made arrangement and church tradition standpoint but from a covenantal and interpretational perspective, no.

All that background and theology to say this: John's Baptism of Repentance, although good and needful, was temporary. Once the nation of Israel rejected the Messiah, the Church was born, and a new baptism, a baptism in the name of the Father, Son and the Holy Ghost replaced the baptism of repentance presented by John the Baptist.

Returning to Acts 19:6, after they were baptized in the name of the Lord Jesus, Paul laid hands on these long previously converted disciples at which time the Holy Spirit came upon them (you could say they were baptized in the Holy Spirit). They subsequently began to speak in a foreign (not gibberish) tongue and even started preaching.

Significantly, the Apostle Paul did not have to pray for them to receive the Holy Spirit (unlike what the Apostles Peter and John demonstrated in Acts 8:15 with the Samaritans). Another important element is that in the Scriptures, we only read of the chosen Apostles having the authority to lay hands on people in connection with the reception of the Holy Spirit.

The Multiple Giving of the Holy Spirit

Of note, Acts 19 becomes the fourth distinct time in the book of Acts (fifth overall) when the Holy Spirit was given. The first instance was in John 20 when Jesus breathed the Holy Spirit unto the ten Apostles. The second instance was in Acts chapter 2, on the Day of Pentecost, and involved the Jews. The third occurrence was in Acts 8, when the Spirit was given to the Samaritans (which were part Jewish) through the laying on of the hands of Peter and John. The fourth instance was in Acts 10, at the household of the Gentile, Cornelius; with the fifth time being here in Acts 19 with the disciples of John's Baptism.

In these five instances, you can say that there were four distinct groups. This is likely why God dealt with them differently for the purpose of translating them into the new church. No doubt it was part of God's plan for setting the foundation of the church. This setting of the church only occurred once...during the lifetime of the apostles. Ephesians 2:20 and I Corinthians 3:10 provide us with this verity.

> And are built upon the foundation of the apostles and prophets, Jesus Christ himself being the chief corner stone; *(Eph 2:20).*

> According to the grace of God which is given unto me, as a wise masterbuilder, I have laid the foundation, and another buildeth thereon. But let every man take heed how he buildeth thereupon. *(1Cor 3:10)*

From this and many other passages, it becomes clear that the foundation of the church was not set by Abraham over 2,100 years before Jesus Christ, Pentecost and the Apostles.

When the disciples of John received the Holy Spirit they spoke with tongues and prophesied. Such supernatural powers were God's method of working in the days before the New Testament was written. As we established previously, every soul that believes in Jesus is baptized with the Holy Spirit.

Without stealing too much from upcoming chapters, what can we then conclude about John the Baptist's "Baptism of Repentance"? Here is a brief listing:

- He was qualified to baptize since he was of Aaron's priestly line. He may have also taken the Nazarite vow since he never drank wine. (If John had taken the vow he would have had long hair. Conversely,

Jesus did not take the Nazarite vow which meant he had short hair.)

- He came in the spirit of the prophet Elijah; the spirit of Elijah being a spirit of truth, of boldness, of zeal and of conviction.

- The prophet Malachi (3:1) prophesied of the coming of John the Baptist as did Isaiah in 40:3-5. John the Baptist spoke Isaiah's very words in Luke 3:4.

  The voice of one crying in the wilderness, Prepare ye the way of the Lord, make his paths straight.

- To prepare the way of the Lord Jesus was meant to set the stage to establishing a simple, straight and narrow path to salvation...a path pleasing God; something that no longer required 613 laws, statutes and commandments.

- John the Baptizer (not John the Christener, nor the sprinkler) would set the stage for Jesus Christ's ministry. He would also set the stage for Holy Spirit and water baptism which were still future during his lifetime.

- He came to assist Jesus in fulfilling all righteousness; to assist in the fulfillment of Scriptures. (Matthew 3:15) A major part of which would be to baptize, to immerse the Messiah in the Jordan River. Only, John was qualified and capable to baptize Jesus the Christ.

- As such, John's baptism of repentance as well as the confessing and forgiveness of sin was to prepare Israel for the Messiah.

- Why? Because the Jews needed the baptism of John to demonstrate "fruits worthy of repentance" (Matthew 3:8) of which John the Baptist's ministry prophetically had to satisfy.

- Like many other feats, works, and doctrines in the Book of Acts, John's Baptism of Repentance is no longer operative for the church age.

In closing, John's Water Baptism bridged the Old Testament Mosaic Law with the Law of Christ: the Law of Liberty. It was a transitional event. John was a bridge. It essentially becomes another facet needed to truly understand Jesus Christ and what He requires of us.

CHAPTER FIVE – WHEN DOES HOLY SPIRIT BAPTISM OCCUR?

> *"The world has hundreds of cultures all of which change year after year. If culture drove the Biblical interpretation then the "truth" behind each verse would be different for a Russian, a Cherokee, a poor person, a rich person, a widow, a divorcee, an orphan, an amputee, an 80 year old, a 20 year old, a rural resident, an urban resident, a freeman, a slave, a Jew, a Gentile, a woman or a man. God wants His disciples to rise above the cultural confusion toward doctrinal purity!"* (Dr. Luis C. Ruiz)

As we continue to explore our subject, we'll be navigating into an area of greater doctrinal complexity as we tackle the aspect of when the Holy Spirit falls on or baptizes a soul. We began addressing this aspect in the last chapter during our study of John's Baptism of Repentance.

Why Some Don't Study In-Depth

Due to the intricate nature of this study, many pastors and teachers either just attach themselves to whatever denominational line they are in or they just plain ole stay away from teaching it. This sad occurrence takes place mostly because of the documented scarcity of Bible reading and theological understanding among Bible teachers across all theological divides.

Interestingly, this author has spoken to several pastors and Bible teachers who state that they stay away from deeper doctrinal teachings because they believe that their congregation or group has not demonstrated an aptitude for digesting what the Bible calls "the meat of the word". Their rationale is that they don't want their spiritually immature congregation to choke on theological meat when they still have not comprehended more basic principles.

Other teachers (right or wrong) believe that many in today's lukewarm churches do not appreciate traditional Bible exposition. They mostly want a "feel-good" message that soothes the itching ear. These "teachers" conveniently skip-over difficult or sensitive messages because they don't want to confuse or God forbid, offend. When that happens, they have joined the ranks of false teachers because they are no longer teaching the complete counsel of God as instructed in the Bible. This author strongly believes that many of these men do not teach deeply because it requires many hours of dedicated study. Most importantly, it requires the leading of the Holy Spirit into all truth.

Certain Biblical themes, like the one we have been exploring, demand interpretational precision and exactness unlike that which is far too-often offered by many theological camps, be they Arminian, Calvinistic or Charismatic. So in order to please God and be obedient, we have to take the Bible at its plain common sense meaning and avoid these broad-brush strokes which are frequently steeped in man-made theological constructs.

In many doctrinally sound congregations, if you were to ask 'when does a soul receive or get baptized by the Holy Spirit or have the Holy Spirit fall on them?' most individuals in those settings would simply conclude 'upon salvation'. Amen to that. However, there are several verses that could appear to contradict this Biblical position if one has either an inconsistent or lazy hermeneutical approach.

In the end, born-again Christians have to really test everything by Scripture. We need to be as noble as those from the church at Berea (Acts 17:10-13). We also have to remember that the Words of God are Spirit, as stated in Ephesians 6:17:

> And take the helmet of salvation, and the sword of the Spirit, which is the word of God.

Our true life (which is our soul) can only truly live by the Words of God as proclaimed by God the Son Himself:

> But he answered and said, It is written, Man shall not live by bread alone, but by every word that proceedeth out of the mouth of God. (Matt 4:4)

We also have to know and understand why we believe what we believe. Otherwise, how will we defend the eternal doctrines of God?

The Breath of God to the Ten

To start our study on when the permanent indwelling of the Holy Spirit takes place we first turn to John 20:21-23. The post-resurrection Jesus is speaking to only ten disciples; for the Apostle Judas had already committed suicide and the unbelieving Apostle Thomas had not yet arrived. Here we read:

> *Then said Jesus to them again, Peace be unto you: as my Father hath sent me, even so send I you. (John 20:21) And when he had said this, he breathed on them, and saith unto them, Receive ye the Holy Ghost: (John 20:22) Whose soever sins ye remit, they are remitted unto them; and whose soever sins ye retain, they are retained. (John 20:23)*
> (See also Genesis 2:7)

These three intriguing verses follow the passage of Jesus telling Mary (likely Magdalene) not to touch Him because He had not yet ascended into heaven to present Himself unto the Father but yet precede the account of Jesus telling the Apostle Thomas to touch His hands and His side.

Focusing on verses 21-22, a question needs to be asked: what does it mean when it states that Jesus Christ breathed on them for them to receive the Holy Ghost? There are several possible interpretations. Some will state, without any Scriptural authority, that Jesus was purely offering a symbolic gesture in that the ten Apostles present did not really receive the Holy Spirit. However, if it were merely symbolic, why would Jesus mislead the disciples?

Others will say that it was merely a foreshadow of what was going to happen at Pentecost such that the Apostles again did not literally receive the Holy Spirit. Following this interpretation, the thought is that Jesus was simply giving a promise of what was going to occur at Pentecost. Some would describe it as sort of a Holy Spirit foretaste or appetizer. Again, Scriptural evidence does not support this view because on other occasions

He decreed the coming of the Holy Spirit without physically breathing on them.

A third explanation states that there was a full outpouring of the Holy Spirit signs and wonders upon the disciples at this time. This seems unlikely in view of such statements given in Luke 24:49 and Acts 1:4-8 where it clearly states that the coming of the full working of the Holy Spirit was still future. This full outpouring view is also doubtful since apostolic signs and wonders did not manifest.

A fourth interpretation states that while these ten Apostles were already saved by faith (which we'll develop later this chapter) the Holy Spirit now indwelled them. What was clearly different was that the Spirit came directly from Jesus' breath, something that will never happen again and only happened once prior.

The only other time that something like that transpired was when the Eternal Jesus (who we're told is the co-creator) breathed the breath of Life into the nostrils of Adam (Genesis 2:7). Thus, Jesus the Christ connects the creation of man with the creation of His church, and to allude that He himself was the author of both works.

Our Lord Jesus here clearly shows us that He is the Giver of both physical and spiritual life. For the reasons already outlined, this method of imparting the Holy Spirit was a one-time event. It was meant to connect two major creations: first, with Adam He creates a living soul within a body; second, with the ten disciples He creates a living Spirit within a body. Remember the soul and the spirit are different as shown by several verses most notably Hebrews 4:12.

> *For the word of God is quick, and powerful, and sharper than any twoedged sword, piercing even to the dividing asunder of soul and spirit, and of the joints and marrow, and is a discerner of the thoughts and intents of the heart.*

Thus, the "breathing out" of the Holy Ghost was meant only for the "believing" Apostles from among those that were chosen. This also sets the stage for the introduction of the Holy Spirit's new ministry of permanently indwelling a person. This then becomes the first giving of the Holy Spirit to the new church. It is appropriate that the only One that is worthy initiated the "new wine" that required "new bottles".

To the Jew at Shavuot

A few weeks later, we read of the second time that the Holy Spirit indwelling was given. During the Feast of Weeks, the Apostle Peter is powerfully preaching to Jewish multitudes that were making one of their three annual pilgrimages to Jerusalem. Let's turn to Acts 2:37 and some of the events at Pentecost to get greater detail.

> *Now when they heard this, they were pricked in their heart, and said unto Peter and to the rest of the apostles, Men and brethren, what shall we do? (Acts 2:37) Then Peter said unto them, <u>Repent, and be baptized every one of you in the name of Jesus Christ for the remission of sins, and ye shall receive the gift of the Holy Ghost.</u> (Acts 2:38) For the promise is unto you, and to your children, and to all that are afar off,*

even as many as the Lord our God shall call. **(Acts 2:39)** *And with many other words did he testify and exhort, saying, Save yourselves from this untoward generation.* **(Acts 2:40)** *Then they that <u>gladly received his word were baptized</u> and the same day there were added unto them about three thousand souls.* **(Acts 2:41)** *And they continued stedfastly in the apostles' doctrine and fellowship, and in breaking of bread, and in prayers.* **(Acts 2:42)** *And fear came upon every soul: and many wonders and signs were done by the apostles.* **(Acts 2:43)** *And all that believed were together, and had all things common;* **(Acts 2:44)**

After repenting, believing and being baptized they had all things in common with the most important commonality being that they were eternally saved by the good news of Jesus Christ.

First, let's establish the overall literary context of the event: Peter was preaching not only to the Jews from Judea and Galilee but also to all of the dispersed Jews living in all of the nations of the known world. Then we are presented with quite possibly one of the more challenging verses dealing with the doctrine of baptism. In verse 38 we read that the Jews needed to repent and be baptized to receive the gift of the Holy Ghost. A question often asked, Is it water baptism or Spirit baptism? Then in verse 40 we're told that:

they that gladly received his word were baptized.

Here the element of faith is added to the equation prior to being baptized. What is clear is that the Jews at Pentecost needed to repent (which is a change of mind accompanied with a desire to change) and believe in Jesus as Messiah.

Two Possible Interpretations?

Two claims could initially be read into this passage for the church age: One is that you must get water baptized to be saved. The other is that one can already be saved prior to being baptized by the Holy Spirit. So if you didn't read the rest of the New Testament, and compare Scripture with Scripture, either of these claims could be correct.

However, when you read and carefully study the rest of the New Testament and see how God continues to reveal His plan during this transitional phase of laying the church foundation then both positions quickly disintegrate. Sort of how theologians who want to believe that the church started with Abraham would have to ignore the verses that state that the Apostles laid the foundation.

Additionally, there are extremely critical elements that we have to keep in mind when interpreting this passage. First, in this instance the baptizing of the Holy Spirit was introduced to the Jews. This becomes pivotal when we start truly studying how the Holy Spirit was unveiled throughout the early church as seen in the book of Acts. That is why some people call this book: the Acts of the Holy Spirit rather than the Acts of the Apostles.

The second element to incorporate into the interpretation is that just like with the Baptism of John overlapping with the church age, the Law of Moses was also overlapping with the Law of Christ. Therefore, it was a transitional period on several fronts.

Some Jews Already Saved by Faith

The third item that is crucial in understanding how the Holy Spirit worked in this particular instance is that many Jews were already saved by faith. They were saved because by faith they believed God's record, God's Words, God's promises etc. And by extension, they were obedient to God's commands as outlined in the Law of Moses. They were saved like: Adam, Abel, Noah, Sarah, Lot, Isaac, Gideon, Moses, Joshua, Rahab and the many others that were saved by faith. All were saved in relation to their faithful heart reaction to the revelation given to them by God.

These faithful and saved Jews now had to believe in God's fulfillment of Old Testament prophecies via God's latest revelation. As a result they believed that Jesus (Yehoshua) was the promised Messiah...the Christ. In effect, it was the next step of progression in their faith in the One and Only true God.

Oppositely, Jews that were not saved by faith via the Old Testament teachings and promises were not inclined to believe in Jesus and His precious Words. Jesus spoke about this very subject in His post-resurrection walk to Emmaus.

> *For had ye believed Moses, ye would have believed me: for he wrote of me. (John 5:46)*
> *But if ye believe not his writings, how shall ye believe my words? (John 5:47)*

59

And in the record (not parable) of Lazarus and the rich man, Jesus finalized the account by stating:

> And he said unto him, If they hear not Moses and the prophets, neither will they be persuaded, though one rose from the dead.
> **(Luke 16:31)**

Although they were chosen...elected by God, many Jews were not saved by faith. They were merely cultural Jews. They were circumcised in the flesh but not circumcised in the heart. As a result, they didn't believe in the resurrection...that Jesus was the Messiah. It was a natural progression of their unbelief.

The Cause or the Result?

All of this background and context is offered in order to present a tenable interpretation of what form of baptism is in view and whether baptism is the cause or the result. Here again are the verses in question:

> ...Repent, and be baptized every one of you in the name of Jesus Christ for the remission of sins, and ye shall receive the gift of the Holy Ghost. **(Acts 2:38)**

> ...gladly received his word were baptized and the same day there were added unto them about three thousand souls. **(Acts 2:41)**

A close reading of verse 38 clearly delineates "baptism" from "receiving the gift of the Holy Ghost". This leaves no other option other than the baptism in verse 38 is referring exclusively to water baptism. Building on this interpretation lends greater clarity to the verse 41 baptism and the proclamation that 3000 souls were baptized after gladly receiving the Truth of

60

Jesus. Given this, we can then assuredly say that water baptism and not Spirit baptism is in view in both verses.

This however can create the issue of adding works (e.g. Water Baptism) to eternal salvation that comes only by faith. Because of this belief, some have adopted the doctrine of baptismal regeneration which requires water baptism as a necessary step to being born-again. Wonderfully, this apparent contradiction vanishes when one incorporates the fact that already saved-by-faith Jews where the ones that believed in Jesus fulfilling the Messianic prophecies. Hence, their salvation was not contingent on their water baptism but rather it was an extension of their already saved position as they were looking for the Messiah. (We covered this aspect in previous pages.) Additionally, there are many scriptural references refuting baptismal regeneration that unmistakably teach that salvation is solely by faith (cf. John 1:12; 3:16; Acts 16:31; Romans 3:21-30; 4:5; 10:9-10; Galatians 2:16; Philippians 3:9).

Introduced Differently

As we will study over the next couple of chapters, the introduction of the Holy Spirit to God's elect (the Jews) at Pentecost was very different than how the Holy Spirit would introduce Himself to other people groups. Thus, what happened in Acts 2 (which is often quoted as if it applies to the church) was different than what unbelieving Gentiles and Jews experience today. Note that we are living long after the transition from under the Mosaic Law to the Law of Christ transpired.

We must also not forget that we have the benefit of the complete canon of 66 inspired, preserved and extant books. We'll be served to remember this reality as we move to the account of the Holy Spirit being given to the Samaritans which holds many similarities to the record of the Jews.

CHAPTER SIX – WHEN DOES HOLY SPIRIT BAPTISM OCCUR? THE SAMARITANS

"The emotional church has encouraged a silent divorce between the Word and the Spirit." (Dr. Luis C. Ruiz)

As we continue with our in-depth look at the Biblical doctrines of baptisms, a review would be beneficial. Last chapter, we ended with the Pentecost arrival of the Holy Spirit found in Acts 2:37-44. After studying the passage, several elements became clear. First, the Apostle Peter was preaching only to Jews. No doubt many of the Jews were from Judea and Galilee with the rest (possibly the majority) being dispersed Jews living in all of the nations of the known world. Even proselyte Jews were included. Overall, these were Jewish men that were making their mandatory pilgrimage to Jerusalem for the Feast of Weeks and were witnesses to the Holy Spirit's new ministry of baptizing believers into the body of Christ. This is one of the several reasons we know that the church started here and not with Abraham, with John the Baptist or at the end of the book of Acts.

We also covered how vital it is to understand that the Holy Spirit baptized into the church Jews that were already saved by faith. They were saved by faith because they believed God's promises and record. They were saved much like the ten Apostles that were already saved by faith and then received the indwelling of the Holy Spirit.

A mistake made by many interpreters and scholars is the false assumption that everyone who received (was baptized by) the Holy Spirit in the book of Acts was not previously saved. In essence, they are transferring the truth of an unsaved Gentile in the church age to an already saved Jew that was part of the transition from the Law to Grace.

As noted beforehand, the Jews at Pentecost were saved no different than Adam, Abel, Noah, Abraham, Sarah, Lot, Isaac, Jacob, Gideon, Moses, Joshua, Rahab and the many others that were saved by faith. The only difference being, that the Acts 2 Jews now believed in God's fulfillment of Old Testament prophecies in contrast to believing in a future fulfillment. It was the next step of progression in their faith of the Mighty Creator God.

To the Samaritan

Proceeding with the third group that received the Holy Ghost, we turn to Acts of the Holy Spirit 8:14-17 for the account of the Samaritans.

Now when the apostles which were at Jerusalem heard that Samaria had received the word of God, they sent unto them Peter and John: (Acts 8:14) Who, when they were come down, prayed for them, that they might receive the Holy Ghost: (Acts 8:15) (For as yet he was fallen upon none of them: only they were baptized in the name of the Lord Jesus.) (Acts 8:16) Then laid they their hands on them, and they received the Holy Ghost. (Acts 8:17)

64

Historical Context

To fully comprehend this passage, one needs to understand who the Samaritans were initially and who they became at this point. So here is some needed background history.

In 931 BC, Israel was divided due to Solomon's and Rehoboam's disobedience. The two tribes in the south retained the name of its largest tribe: Judah (Jerusalem being its capital). The ten northern tribes retained the name Israel for their country. At times Israel was also identified in the Bible as Ephraim, Manasseh or Joseph due to them being the larger and more influential of the ten northern tribes.

Throughout its 209 year history, the Northern Kingdom had several capitals. Built by Jeroboam, its first two capitals were Shechem and Penuel. Some twenty years later, King Baasha selected the ancient and aesthetically beautiful city of Tirzah as its capital. Two kings later, the evil King Omri purchased a hill which in the Hebrew was called "Sha-mer-own" (named after its owner "Shemer"). This hill "Sha-mer-own" eventually gets transliterated into English as 'Samaria'. King Omri then constructed on this hilltop of Samaria and in his sixth year (about 50 years after the split from the south) he moved the capital from Tirzah to Samaria. Over time, as the northern kingdom of Israel (and its ten tribes) became more apostate, more idolatrous and more wicked they began to be called by the name of its capital city, Samaria. Hence, you had both the capital city and its country known as Samaria with its people known as Samaritans.

Samaria became closely associated as a demonic high place of Baal worship such that a house/palace was built for this satanic deity right within its city limits. They had even developed an extensive professional class of Baal priests to "serve" the evil desires of the people. Scripture informs us that part of their motivation for having their own place of worship along with the priests was to dissuade its citizens from congregating and worshipping in Jerusalem.

Baal worship consisted of: the worship of demon gods and their representative idols (this of course included the adoration and reverence of the sun, moon and stars.). It also included infant sacrifices, all manners of sexual deviancy and the conjuring up of the dead to name a few. Even in the midst of all of this evil, the Samaritans still kept some of their Jewish beliefs and traditions. Like many churches of today, the Samaritans mixed some truth with much error. This is called syncretism, and it is how Satan corrupts godly things while giving its practitioners a false illusion that they are worshipping God in truth. Sadly, this has been and still is pervasive throughout "Christianity".

This depravity in worship continued until God sent the Assyrians to destroy and disperse the Northern Kingdom due to their wickedness. Thus, the country of Samaria continued as a self-governing nation until it was conquered by Assyria in 722 BC.

Fast forwarding to the times of Jesus and the Apostles, we read of a reestablished Samaria; this time not as a sovereign nation but as a sub-region under the rule of the Roman Empire. Here we find that the Jews have completely separated themselves from the Samaritans such that they didn't interact or even speak to them. That is why the parable of the Good Samaritan was such an offense to self-righteous Jews.

Separation: Good & Bad

As an aside, it is important to note that the Bible actually supports a healthy doctrine of separation as well as condemns unbiblical doctrine separation. The Jews were correct in separating themselves from the evil and apostate Samaritan practices but wrong in completely shunning the Samaritans and viewing them as lesser people. Often, Scripture provides the only truth and refuge from heresies that stem from two extremes. This "two extremes view" can also be called a "False Dichotomy" because people errantly believe that there are only two viable options to select. Equally dangerous is the tactic of creating a compromise view from the two extremes which is called a "Hegelian Dialectic". Bottom-line is that God's truth must only come from His Word not from intellectual or emotional ploys. Much more can be said about these evil tactics but we will leave that for another treatise.

Notwithstanding, the Samaritans could still claim kinship with the Jew since they both considered Jacob as their Father (John 4:12). By extension, many Samaritans could also claim Joseph as their ancestral father, as well as either of his sons: Ephraim and Manasseh.

So even though they had been compromised centuries earlier and were mostly living in spiritual darkness, the Samaritans still had just enough light of God's Old Testamental truths and promises to believe that a Deliverer/Saviour would come to Earth. Some

Samaritans believed that Jesus was that very Saviour. That truth is told to us in John 4:39-42:

> And many of the Samaritans of that city believed on him for the saying of the woman, which testified, He told me all that ever I did. *(John 4:39)* So when the Samaritans were come unto him, they besought him that he would tarry with them: and he abode there two days. *(John 4:40)* And many more believed because of his own word; *(John 4:41)* And said unto the woman, Now we believe, not because of thy saying: for we have heard him ourselves, and know that this is indeed the Christ, the Saviour of the world. *(John 4:42)*

No Threefold Division of the Law

While authentic Samaritans could still claim being physiological Jews, they long lost the ability to claim being Spiritual Jews. Spiritual Jews were those that would worship the only true God and that would be obedient to the 613 Mosaic Laws. It is beneficial to note that unlike what mainstream Christian pundits teach, there is no such thing as a three-part division of the law (Moral, Ceremonial and Civil). This three-part division is actually an anti-Biblical man-made teaching that creates all sorts of confusion and division. Nowhere in Scripture is the Mosaic Law divided in this fashion. Rather, we're told by Jesus and the Apostles that the Law was one unit, and that if you break one law you were guilty of breaking all of them.

For whosoever shall keep the whole law, and yet offend in one point, he is guilty of all. **(James 2:10)**

For as many as are of the works of the law are under the curse: for it is written, Cursed is every one that continueth not in all things which are written in the book of the law to do them. **(Gal 3:10)**

Whosoever therefore shall break one of these least commandments, and shall teach men so, he shall be called the least in the kingdom of heaven: but whosoever shall do and teach them, the same shall be called great in the kingdom of heaven. **(Matt 5:19)**

Returning to the Samaritans, the John 4 and Acts 8 passages clearly express that they were a completely separate people group that was next in-line to be baptized in the Holy Spirit. They were really a sort of an apostate Jew. They were considered worse than Gentiles by the Spiritual Jew because they had been exposed to God's complete truth but chose the way of Baal and demonism.

Notwithstanding, God loved the Samaritans just the same as He initially sent the deacon/evangelist Philip to preach the good news of Jesus Christ (Acts 8). Similar to the remnant Jews, there were Samaritans that were expectant of the Messiah as was prophesied in the Torah. At this point in the early church, we're told that the Samaritans believed that Jesus was the Messiah. We read that those saved individuals then willingly chose to be immersed via water baptized.

69

It was after that that God then sent the chosen Apostles Peter and John into Samaria to lay hands on them in order to receive the Holy Ghost. It is here (Acts 8) that we read of the third distinct manner (out of five) in which the Holy Spirit landed on different groups of people.

As you recall, we first read how Jesus breathed on the ten already saved Apostles to receive the Holy Spirit. Second, we read that repentance was a requirement of Holy Spirit Baptism among the already saved Spiritual Jew. Only now to be followed by the example of the mixed peoples called the Samaritans.

The Ordering of the Samaritan Reception

The Lord Jesus introduced the permanent sealing of the Holy Spirit to the already saved apostles, and now Christ's Apostles were used to introduce Holy Spirit baptism, indwelling and sealing to the Jew first (Acts 2) and now the Samaritan (Acts 8). Lets' re-read the passage:

> Now when the apostles which were at Jerusalem heard that Samaria had received the word of God, they sent unto them Peter and John: *(Acts 8:14)* Who, when they were come down, prayed for them, that they might receive the Holy Ghost: *(Acts 8:15)* (For as yet he was fallen upon none of them: only they were baptized in the name of the Lord Jesus.) *(Acts 8:16)* Then laid they their hands on them, and they received the Holy Ghost. *(Acts 8:17)*

Notice the order for the Samaritans: First, they received/believed the Gospel of Jesus Christ. This means they were saved. This is exactly the same as occurred with the Jews at Pentecost. Second, they were water baptized in the name of the Lord Jesus. This is also similar to the Jews as they were water baptized.

Next, Peter and John prayed and laid hands upon the Samaritans. They had to physically go the Samaritan people...they couldn't do it remotely. So just like the Apostles were used to usher in the Holy Spirit's new ministry of indwelling/sealing to the Jews, they would have to be used to open the door to Holy Spirit baptism to the Samaritans.

If someone only read this passage and walked away from the Bible, they would believe that to get baptized by the Holy Spirit first you would need to trust in Jesus, then be baptized by water then have an apostle lay hands on you. Only then would you be baptized by the Holy Spirit into the body of Christ. Sadly, there are churches and pastors that have adopted this approach not realizing that they are trying to implement a practice that doesn't apply to today's unsaved Gentile but rather was only used to lay the foundation of the church with the Samaritans.

With these errant doctrines, you could believe that you could be saved and not be Holy Spirit baptized. You could also believe that someone needs to lay hands on you to receive the Holy Spirit. You could even believe that you needed faith and water baptism prior to being Holy Spirit baptized. All of these damnable teachings create chaos and place unbiblical burdens on people seeking to worship the True God. The enemy of our souls is pleased when this occurs!

Do they apply to the Church?

The question is, can the church claim any of these first three Spirit baptisms as applying today? Many already know the answer. But for those still struggling, we'll find out more over the next couple of chapters when we cover the final two Holy Spirit baptism groupings. With God's leading, we'll clearly determine what we should believe and how to be obedient in this church age.

For now, let's reintroduce one clear passage:

*For by one Spirit are we **all** baptized into one body, whether we be Jews or Gentiles, whether we be bond or free; and have been **all** made to drink into one Spirit.* **(1Cor 12:13)**

All are baptized into the body of Christ by one Spirit. All Christians are made to drink into one Spirit. So while there are different levels of rewards, crowns and inheritances for believers they all have equal access to God's complete power that resides inside of them. It is only when we rightly divide the Word of Truth, that can we determine how God wants us to worship Him and how we can be obedient.

One Lord, one faith, one baptism, **(Eph 4:5)**

CHAPTER SEVEN – WHEN DOES HOLY SPIRIT BAPTISM OCCUR? THE GENTILES & THE ISOLATED JEWS

"We must strive for unity but never at the expense of Truth." (Dr. Luis C. Ruiz)

Continuing our study on when does Holy Spirit baptism occurs, let's quickly review the first three occasions. The initial record occurred in John 20 where we read how the resurrected Jesus Christ breathed the Holy Spirit into His ten believing Jewish Apostles. In Acts 2, we studied the arrival of the Holy Spirit to the assembled Jews at the annual feast of weeks (Shavuot). In this case, Peter was the chief instrument used by God. Then in Acts 8, we examined how the Holy Spirit fell upon another unique group: the Samaritans where we read that Peter and John had to lay hands to summons the Holy Ghost.

While these above passages were written for our learning, it was very clear that the passages were not written for us to emulate; for we are neither the ten saved Apostles, nor the saved Jews and nor Samaritans awaiting a Messiah. In all three instances, we read and confirmed that the Holy Spirit baptized souls at different moments and only after distinctive works/manifestations.

At this juncture, some readers may still be struggling with piecing together some of the doctrinal elements. Don't fret. In the following chapter, all five Holy Spirit launching instances will be compared. Once all five are presented, we'll Biblically sort out what applies to us: the church. We will also navigate through "proof passages" that are erroneously used to support inaccurate renderings of Holy Spirit baptism.

To illustrate, let's use a car mechanic metaphor. Many mechanics tear apart an engine (placing all the parts in front of them) in order to put it back together again in perfect working condition. When this is done, the mechanic develops an intimate knowledge of how an engine works. Similarly, when a Christian breaks down the Bible (placing all the verses in front of them) they'll better interpret the Bible and understand what Jesus Christ desires from their life.

At this point, let's inject some more baptismal levity.

> After his Baptism at church, little 8 year old Billy sobbed all the way home in the back seat of the car. His father asked him three times what was wrong. Finally, Billy replied, 'The pastor said he that he was glad that I was going to be raised in a Christian home, but I want to stay with you guys.'

To the Gentile

Now we turn to the passage when the Holy Spirit was received by the Gentiles in Acts 10:44-48 and its retelling in Acts 11:15-18.

> While Peter yet spake these words, the Holy Ghost fell on all them which heard the word. (Acts 10:44) And they of the circumcision which believed were astonished, as many as came with Peter, because that on the Gentiles also was poured out the gift of the

Holy Ghost. (Acts 10:45) For they heard them speak with tongues, and magnify God. Then answered Peter, (Acts 10:46) Can any man forbid water, that these should not be baptized, which have received the Holy Ghost as well as we? (Acts 10:47) And he commanded them to be baptized in the name of the Lord. Then prayed they him to tarry certain days. (Acts 10:48)

And as I began to speak, the Holy Ghost fell on them, as on us at the beginning. (Acts 11:15) Then remembered I the word of the Lord, how that he said, John indeed baptized with water; but ye shall be baptized with the Holy Ghost. (Acts 11:16) Forasmuch then as God gave them the like gift as he did unto us, who believed on the Lord Jesus Christ; what was I, that I could withstand God? (Acts 11:17) When they heard these things, they held their peace, and glorified God, saying, Then hath God also to the Gentiles granted repentance unto life. (Acts 11:18)

In these accounts, the Apostle Peter is mightily used by God to once again introduce the Holy Spirit to a third people group: this time the Gentiles. As the Apostle preached salvation through Jesus Christ only, this group of Gentiles believed on the message of salvation only through Jesus.

We're told the very moment that they believed on the Lord Jesus they were baptized with the Holy Spirit. We're told that only after willingly accepting the free gift (believing) did God give them the gift of the Holy

Spirit. The same like gift that was given to the Jews and the Samaritans.

In this particular instance, Holy Spirit baptism was followed by the newly saved speaking in a foreign language/tongue, no doubt to witness to other non-believers. This is the true purpose of speaking in another known language. (1 Corinthians 14:22)

> *Wherefore tongues are for a sign, not to them that believe, but to them that believe not: but prophesying serveth not for them that believe not, but for them which believe.*

As a testimony of their new found faith and as an act of obedience, the Gentiles were shortly thereafter freely water baptized, immersed in the name of the Lord. Yet another passage that clearly separates what is salvation by faith and the subsequent act of water baptism. (Acts 11:17)

It is also a passage that clearly refutes infant or paedo baptism as we are told that they believed; something that an infant cannot do. (This includes infants living with saved parents.) It's also worth noting that the Jews were astonished at this happening to the Gentiles...more so than it happening to the Samaritans.

Not Merely an Addition to the Torah

If you continue reading the account of Acts you will see that the introduction of the Gentiles into God's plan of salvation wrought havoc in the Jewish false notion that faith in Jesus Christ and the permanent baptism of the Holy Spirit was merely an addition to the Law of Moses. Many were not aware that this new revelation actually satisfied the Mosaic Law.

They eventually had to come to grips that they were no longer under the Mosaic Law but under grace. This is spoken about by our Master when He told the Jews that they could no longer put new wine into old bottles. (Matthew 9:17; Mark 2:22) Sadly, the error of the Judaizers via the merging of law and grace; the fusing of the 613 Mosaic Laws with the Law of Liberty still occurs today with several religious groups such as the SDA, Mainline Denominations and Roman Catholicism.

Now we come to our fifth and last example of Holy Spirit Baptism. For this example, we return to the passage that we studied earlier in the book when we considered the "Baptism of John the Baptist" in Acts 19. In this chapter, we will analyze it focusing on the Spirit baptism aspect versus the water baptism perspective.

> *He said unto them, Have ye received the Holy Ghost since ye believed? And they said unto him, We have not so much as heard whether there be any Holy Ghost. (Acts 19:2) And he said unto them, Unto what then were ye baptized? And they said, Unto John's baptism. (Acts 19:3) Then said Paul, John verily baptized with the baptism of repentance, saying unto the people, that they should believe on him which should come after him, that is, on Christ Jesus. (Acts 19:4) When they heard this, they were baptized in the name of the Lord Jesus. (Acts 19:5) And when Paul had laid his hands upon them, the Holy Ghost came on them; and they spake with tongues, and prophesied. (Acts 19:6)*

Isolated but True Believers

Something about the Apostle Paul's interaction with these disciples in Ephesus alerted him to inquire, "Did you receive the Holy Spirit when you believed?" The response from these Jewish disciples was essentially that they had not heard of the Holy Spirit. Then notice how the Apostle Paul affirms them as believers...never questioning their faith or their saved position in Jesus Christ.

Along those lines, some incorrectly interpret that these disciples were unbelievers despite the fact that Paul asserts the opposite. And why can we say this confidently? Because we have already read of two clear examples of believers who did not receive the Holy Spirit immediately on belief: the Samaritans who awaited the arrival of Peter and John (Acts 8:12-17) as well as the Jewish believers on the Day of Pentecost (Acts 1:4-5; 2:1-4).

The Apostle Paul having perfect doctrine revealed to him by Jesus Christ, as well as the Holy Spirit, knew the exact follow-up question to them not knowing about the Holy Spirit. He states, *Unto what then were ye baptized?*" It was an open-ended question (without any leading) to get to the bottom of the issue.

If Paul would have used a closed-ended question approach, he may have alternatively asked, "Did you get water baptized under John's baptism of repentance?" (Many Jews had already submitted to John's Baptism.) Or "Did you get water-baptized in the name of the Lord Jesus?" (This occurred several times in the book of Acts.)

These disciples responded, *"We have been baptized unto John's baptism"*. Hence, the extent of their knowledge was that the Messiah had still not arrived, and they had signified their repentance via the baptism of John as a necessary step of preparation for receiving Him as King. Their hearts were already prepared; they were just awaiting the Messiah's arrival (albeit many years after Jesus' ascension).

Paul recognizing the significance of John's baptism as preparatory for the nation of Israel and their promised messianic kingdom affirms: *"John indeed baptized with a baptism of repentance"*. Recall that their answer *"Unto John's baptism"* shows why they had not yet received the Spirit. They had only submitted to John's baptism.

Directed by the Holy Spirit, the Apostle Paul likely explained how the Christ had come, died, been buried, had risen from the dead, had ascended back to heaven, and that He had sent the Holy Spirit at Pentecost. He reminded them that when John baptized with the baptism of repentance, the Baptist also urged them to believe on the coming Christ.

Notice here again how the Scriptures differentiate between repentance and belief, thus rendering each distinguishable. We will not focus on that in this work but understanding the difference between faith and repentance as well as how they work together is crucial to grasping the book of Acts and the Good News of Jesus.

In verse 5 we read that once they heard this, they realized that they still lacked the water baptism that identified them with the Body of Christ and so they immediately were water baptized in the name of the Lord Jesus. As discussed previously, John's baptism, although good and necessary for the Jews, was temporary...a bridge. Entrance into the newly formed church required a new baptism...a baptism that identified them as part of the Body of Christ.

Then in verse 6 we come upon another often misunderstood, misinterpreted verse where we are told that these believing disciples (that had already been baptized in the name of Jesus Christ) received the baptism of the Holy Spirit only after the Apostle lays hands on them. This showcased (more than anything) how only the chosen Apostles of Christ had authority to lay hands on people in connection with the reception of the Holy Spirit.

Unlike in the case of the Samaritans, Paul did not have to pray with these disciples of John the Baptist in order to receive the Spirit baptism. And on top of it all, these disciples immediately started speaking in other languages and prophesied after receiving the baptism of the Holy Spirit. This passage of course is one focused on by certain groups at the expense of ignoring the other Scriptures.

Confusion in the Body

So here we have the fifth distinct time (fourth in the book of Acts) where the Holy Spirit was received; each being preceded by a unique or different ordering of events. Sadly, these unique events and ordering have caused confusion and division in the body of Christ for hundreds of years. Unfortunately, often when people take a doctrinal position...pick a doctrinal team per se, their pride, or their family, or their livelihood, or their denomination selfishly stops them from seeking Truth and admitting their error. This is the main culprit of the many divisions in Christianity.

If we read the Bible we can clearly know certain attributes of God's eternal character.

> *For God is not the author of confusion, but of peace, as in all churches of the saints.* **(1Cor 14:33)**

By extension, we know that there is order, not just in heaven but also reflected in the local church.

> *For this cause left I thee in Crete, that thou shouldest set in order the things that are wanting, and ordain elders in every city, as I had appointed thee:* **(Titus 1:5)**

> *Let **all** things be done decently and in order.* **(1Cor 14:40)**

This order in the local church also extends to doctrinal purity.

> *Now I beseech you, brethren, mark them which cause divisions and offences contrary to the doctrine which ye have learned; and avoid them.* **(Romans 16:17)**

Not surprisingly, this doctrinal purity and oneness is important to God.

> *How is it then, brethren? when ye come together, every one of you hath a psalm, hath a doctrine, hath a tongue, hath a revelation, hath an interpretation. Let all things be done unto edifying.* **(1Cor 14:26)**

So now that all the pieces of puzzle are on the table, in the upcoming chapters we will decently set them in order. This is done so that everyone isn't walking around with their own personal doctrine such that through their error they cause needless division and offences. It is then that local bodies of Christ can come together in the power of the Holy Spirit. Biblical unity can only come with truth!

CHAPTER EIGHT – WHEN DOES HOLY SPIRIT BAPTISM OCCUR? THE COMPARISON

"Just one verse in God's Holy Words can provoke innumerable views, can elicit untold opinions and can stir immeasurable emotions but none of these regardless of how eloquent or seemingly persuasive can alter God's immutable Truth!" (Dr. Luis C. Ruiz)

In the previous chapters, it was clearly seen how God worked uniquely with different people groups as He established His body of believers. In addition, we identified five unique and distinct events in the early church related to how the Holy Spirit introduced His baptizing and indwelling ministry to mankind. As such, these teachings clearly fall into the area of Scriptural meat and not milk.

In this chapter, we will review those five distinct events and set them in proper order. We'll thereby attempt putting together the puzzle into an airtight, ironclad doctrinal position that you can confidently hold onto and share with others.

The Importance of Studying Scripture

Prior to progressing in our study there are a couple of items that we still need to address in order to connect the puzzle pieces. We'll do this by way of the question, why is this study or for that matter any doctrinal study important? The correct response being, that God requires us to study His Words in order to establish sound doctrine that will enable Christians to obey God and worship Him in a manner that brings Him glory.

Oppositely, what happens when we don't properly understand His Words? Stated differently, what are some of the potential consequences of not understanding His Words?

- Not understanding the Bible is why people baptize infants. Some following Romanist doctrines believe that non-baptized babies actually go to a place they call purgatory. (BTW – Purgatory is a non-existent place that the Bible calls a damnable doctrine because it wrongly declares that a damned soul in purgatory can actually be freed to heaven by prayers and gift offerings to the church.) Also, baptized infants eventually turn into adults having a false sense of security in heaven because they were sprinkled many years prior.

- Not understanding the Bible is why Romanism has baptized unbelieving men and women in order to join a church without faith...without being born-again. This corrupts the faith and also gives souls a false sense of eternal security with God in heaven.

- Not understanding the Bible makes people sprinkle and pour instead of immersing, thereby omitting that water baptism is a figure of Christ's death, burial and resurrection.

- Not understanding the Bible makes people believe that you are saved only after being water baptized; ignoring many passages and adding works to salvation. This becomes true legalism and has kept many in spiritual bondage.

- Not understanding the Bible makes some believe that people will receive the Holy Spirit by the laying of hands as done by Jesus' chosen Apostles.

- Not understanding the Bible is why people believe that Holy Spirit baptism is a second work or a second blessing that comes subsequent to salvation.

- Not understanding the Bible make some believe that you will speak in undecipherable gibberish upon receiving the Holy Spirit.

- Not understanding the Bible is why people teach that after believing in Christ you have to stop sinning in certain areas in order to get water baptized. This has stunted the spiritual growth of many.

- Not understanding the Bible makes people believe that being water baptized is not important to God and not necessary to their growth in Christ.

For these and many other reasons it is important to connect the dots by comparing Scripture with Scripture and to establish sound and provable doctrine. All of this is essential to God. Otherwise, how can you, I, we please God if we're doing something or expecting something or teaching something that is contrary to God's will.

> *There is a way which seemeth right unto a man, but the end thereof are the ways of death.* **(Proverbs 14:12)**

Each Instance Unique

At this juncture we'll do one last analysis of the five distinct times and ways that the Holy Spirit was received.

85

For the ten non-doubting Jewish Apostles in John 20:22 the order was:

- Already saved by faith/belief in God's Old Testament Law and Promises.
- The ten believed that the risen Jesus was the prophesied Christ.
- Received the Holy Spirit via Jesus' breath

For the Jewish believer in Acts 2 the order was:

- Already saved by faith/belief in God's Old Testament Law and Promises. (An untold amount could have partaken in John's water baptism of repentance.)
- Repentance.
- Water Baptism in the name of the Lord Jesus.
- Reception/Baptism of the Holy Spirit.

These Jews already believed in Moses and the prophets so it was not asked for at Pentecost. Since faith in the coming Messiah was already present only repentance was required.

For the Samaritans in Acts 8:14–17 the following events occurred:

- Faith in Jesus Christ as the Messiah via the Apostle Philip's preaching.
- Water baptism in the name of the Lord Jesus.
- The Apostles prayed for them.
- The Apostles laid their hands on them.
- Reception/Baptism of the Holy Spirit.

For the Gentiles in Acts 10:44–48 their conversion is in view. The order here was:

- Faith in Jesus Christ
- Reception/Baptism of the Holy Spirit

- Water baptism in the name of the Lord Jesus

A final community of believers is made up of Jewish disciples of John the Baptist, Acts 19:1-7:

- Faith in Jesus as Messiah.
- Water re-baptism.
- The Apostle Paul laid his hands on them.
- Reception of the Holy Spirit.

Which Applies to us?

Can any one of these five conditions apply to us...the body of Christ? To answer this question, let's further break down the occurrences and go through a process of elimination.

First, it is clear that not all apply for today for several reasons. They are:

1) They all targeted different groupings of individuals.

2) God is a God of order and He clearly has not communicated that all five are active for the church especially when they are all different and at times contradict one another.

3) These unique Holy Spirit baptisms were all initiated by Jesus' chosen Apostles and all occurred during the setting of the foundation of the church. As conveyed by 1 Corinthians 3:10:

   According to the grace of God which is given unto me, as a wise masterbuilder, I have laid the foundation, and another buildeth thereon. But let every man take heed how he buildeth thereupon.

This verse as well as Ephesians 2:20 effectively eliminates the incarnate Jesus Christ personally breathing into us the Holy Spirit (option 1). As we discussed previously, this only happened when God created Adam and when He created the church via the Spirit's dwelling.

Turning to option 2 at the day of Pentecost in Acts 2, a couple of facts would eliminate that sequence for today. First, you have to remember that the Jews at Pentecost were already saved by faith much like the Apostles. They were faithful Jews that observed the Mosaic Law which was simply a "shadow of things to come" (Colossians 2:16-17) and a "schoolmaster to Christ". (Galatians 3:24)

Another aspect that would eliminate option 2 is that if you held to what occurred at Pentecost to be applicable today, you could only receive the Holy Spirit after you were immersed/baptized in water which is a grave heresy. This would mean that some believers would be sealed by the Holy Spirit while others would not be sealed.

Let's not forget that the manner which the Holy Spirit baptized the Jews contradicts the manner in which the Holy Spirit came to the Gentiles in Acts 10 and 11. We should also remember that Paul did not focus on water baptism which would have been strange if one's salvation depended on it. 1 Corinthians 1:17 reads:

For Christ sent me not to baptize, but to preach the gospel: not with wisdom of words, lest the cross of Christ should be made of none effect.

Thus, we can confidently eliminate option 2 (the Holy Spirit at Pentecost) as being active for today.

Now let's move to the third option; the Holy Spirit baptism involving the Samaritans. As we have studied, the Samaritans were a distinct people group; not quite Jewish...not quite Gentile. You could almost categorize them as apostate Jews. Nevertheless God loved them and wanted to draw them to Himself. Jesus spoke of them on a couple of occasions.

As such, God orchestrated a unique manner of drawing the Samaritans to Him. To begin with, He used the Holy-Spirit filled Deacon/Evangelist Philip to preach the Gospel of Christ. In God's power, Philip wrought miracles among the Samaritans to lay the ground work. We're then told in Acts 8 that many Samaritans believed in Christ and that numerous unclean spirits departed the once possessed souls of Samaria.

This was no small feat given that much of Samaria was bewitched (today we call it being under a curse that could include hypnosis or mesmerization) by a witch sorcerer named Simon. However, the Acts record tells us that the witch Simon also believed in Christ and that along with all of the Samaritans that believed were baptized in water in the name of Jesus but yet no Holy Spirit.

It is then that we read of God sending Peter and John to do the final close on the Samaritans. On this occasion, the Apostles prayed and laid hands on the Samaritans after which they received the fullness of the Holy Spirit. Hence, the foundation was laid with those in Samaria.

Much like the Jewish option, we must not be induced into thinking that the Samaritan experience is for the church age. Again, the Apostles were used to pray, lay-hands and set the foundation. This was exclusively an apostolic work that cannot be replicated today. And like the event at Pentecost with the Jews, it disconnects salvation from Holy Spirit baptism. Hence, the Samaritan Holy Spirit experience along with Peter, John and Philip is not for today.

Skipping the fourth option for now and addressing the fifth option, we find that God used the Apostle Paul in a miraculously unique manner. As we studied previously, Paul comes across a group of disciples that had only experienced the Baptism of John. Much like the Apostles and the Jewish believers at Pentecost, these disciples were saved without the Holy Spirit.

Paul is then used to preach the Gospel of Christ of which they wholly believed. We then read how they we're re-baptized in the name of Jesus. Afterwards, Paul lays hands on them and they subsequently were baptized in the Holy Spirit.

Candidly, what makes the Bible sometimes difficult to interpret is that there are often overlaps in the different covenants or economies or dispensations of the Bible. In this case, there was a significant lag before everyone had heard the Gospel of Jesus Christ...of Him dying and resurrecting. Paul eventually caught up with this unique outlier group quite possibly 20 to 25 years after the resurrection.

As with the other discussed options, the unique events surrounding the Holy Spirit baptism of those that had only received the Baptism of John is not for today. The 66 book canon is closed. The information about Jesus has disseminated...no one is need of the next revealed step. We have all that we need right here and now.

The Winner

This takes us back to option four...our victor...what applies to today's church. Why? In view in this option is Peter's experience with the Gentiles in Acts 10-11. The pattern for reception of the Holy Spirit during the church age is set: belief in Jesus being the Christ, the Son of God accompanied with the immediate reception of the Holy Spirit. Here, salvation and Holy Spirit baptism are linked.

This link between salvation and Holy Spirit baptism comes without water baptism, without laying of hands, without tongues, without any other work. However, if we are in obedience, water baptism should then soon follow. To confirm this, we again turn to Ephesians 4:4-5:

> *There is one body, and one Spirit, even as*
> *ye are called in one hope of your calling;*
> *One Lord, one faith, one baptism.*

One Holy Spirit baptism at salvation which seals your salvation and initiates you into the living organism called the church...the "ecclesia" in Greek.

Another confirmation comes from that fact that in the church age God is also calling out of the Gentiles a people for His Name. This passage found in Acts 15:14 which occurs after God baptized the Jews and the Samaritans. The Bible also tells us that God is focused on three people groups which are the Jews, the Gentiles and the church. (1 Corinthians 10:32)

> *Give none offence, neither to the Jews, nor to the Gentiles, nor to the church of God:*

In summation, the only Biblical order for the post apostolic church is that which simultaneously occurs. They are: **Born** of the Spirit, **Baptized** of the Spirit, **Indwelt** of the Spirit and **Sealed** by the Spirit (Ephesians 1:12-13). The only thing that occurs after salvation, if we are obediently seeking God, is being filled by the Holy Spirit. That is what God commands for all of us and becomes our next topic.

CHAPTER NINE – THE FILLING OF THE HOLY GHOST

"The plain truth is once we leave the Scriptures (66 books) anyone can say anything and believe anything and do anything. This has irreverently thrusted God into post-modern relativism. Hence there are no absolutes...nothing is certain. This spirit has infiltrated the church." (Dr. Luis C. Ruiz)

The next topic of examination is technically not about the doctrine of baptisms. However, it needs to be discussed because it often gets confused with Holy Spirit baptism. As such, this chapter will cover the amazing topic of being filled with the Holy Spirit.

This filling, which comes to us as a gift of obeying and resting in Christ, is something that all Christians should pray and yearn for in their lives. While doing works for God is a wonderful thing, this Holy Spirit filling only comes from a person decreasing and allowing God to increase in their life. We have to remember that God will not force us to decrease. He may place barriers and obstacles in our life, but in the end, much like Jonah and Job, the submission has to occur willingly.

Difference Between Filling & Baptism

Ephesians 5:18-19 is the standard starting point to begin a study on Holy Spirit filling.

And be not drunk with wine, wherein is excess; but be filled with the Spirit; Speaking to yourselves in psalms and hymns and spiritual songs, singing and making melody in your heart to the Lord;

Here and in other verses, the Bible clearly delineates between the "Filling of the Spirit" and the "Baptism of the Holy Spirit". Except in those unique instances where the Holy Spirit is introduced to certain people groups (which we just covered) the believer is not commanded to be baptized with the Spirit, but rather he is commanded to be filled with the Spirit. Therefore, unlike being baptized in the Holy Spirit (which God never commands), God commands all believers of the church age to "be filled with the Holy Spirit".

It is interesting to note, God offers the illustration of one being under the control of alcohol to exemplify that a Christian should let himself be controlled by the Holy Spirit. Similar to alcohol or wine controlling words, behaviors and thoughts, the Holy Spirit filled soul is one controlled by God. Thus, the phrase "filled with the Spirit" connotes "to be under the influence of".

There are several examples in the New Testament of a believer's soul being filled with the Spirit.

1. In Acts 4:8, Peter was *"filled with the Holy Ghost"* as he preached.

2. In Acts 6:3, the most important qualification for the first deacons was they needed to be men *"full of the Holy Ghost and wisdom"*.

3. In Acts 6:5 and 7:55, Stephen, was *"full of faith and the Holy Spirit"* up until his death by stoning.

4. In Acts 11:24, Barnabas was *"full of the Spirit"*.

The Greek verb translated into filled is "pleh-roh'-o". Its synonyms are: fill; fulfil; be full; complete; ended; perfect. An interesting translation of "pleh-roh'-o" is found in Philippians 4:19.

> *But my God shall <u>supply</u> all your need according to his riches in glory by Christ Jesus.*

Here, the Authorized Version (AV) authors use "supply" instead of the commonly used verbs of "fill" or "fulfil" while yet retaining its broader meaning.

Ephesians 3:17-19 is another passage that addresses being filled while using the same Greek word.

> *That Christ may dwell in your hearts by faith; that ye, being rooted and grounded in love, (Eph 3:17) May be able to comprehend with all saints what is the breadth, and length, and depth, and height; (Eph 3:18) And to know the love of Christ, which passeth knowledge, that ye might be <u>filled</u> with all the <u>fulness</u> of God. (Eph 3:19)*

Again, we note that God desires His children to be always filled with His fulness. However, God's grace of Spirit Filling is only realized when a believer fully surrenders to Christ in that moment. It is critical to remember that Paul is writing to solely to believers; hence it is a post salvation experience.

When is a Soul Filled with the Spirit?

A question often asked is: "how does one know they are filled with the Holy Spirit?" This author's response comes from experiences in preaching, teaching, one-on-one evangelism and even by way of writing. In all of these cases, it was apparent that God took control.

When Spirit filled, in some cases, you may not remember saying things that blessed others; speaking words that were far beyond your own ability such that you would never be able to re-produce what was done or said. There is an effortlessness...a sense where you are not really working; only God is working. These are the times that the Holy Spirit has clearly taken over.

In those precious moments, we are completely resting in Jesus Christ and have a confidence; an assurance that the results and consequences are His and His alone. Other times, many of us will want to be the center of attention, take the credit, drive our own ideas rather than having the Holy Spirit filling and leading us. It is at those times, that we own the results and consequences: good or bad.

Along those lines, many people believe that they are worshipping God in spirit when in reality they are worshipping from their soul. Worshipping in soul is very different because the Bible considers it fleshly and is typically emotionally and/or intellectually centered. In these occasions, God is certainly not glorified.

Oppositely, worshipping in the Spirit is actually letting God's Spirit take front and center while at the same time, taming our soulish emotions. In this instance, God receives the glory and the believer the blessing. Fascinatingly, the Bible has much to say about the separation of the soul and the spirit. (Watchman Nee's work "The Spiritual Man" details many of the Biblical contrasts of the spirit and the soul.)

Two Natures

Letting oneself be filled with the Spirit is also a reference to the fact that the Christian has two natures. One is the old or carnal nature and the other is the new or spiritual nature. (Romans 6 and 7) The Christian can let himself be controlled by the old or carnal self that comes with sin (1 John 1:8-10), or can allow the Holy Spirit who indwells him...to control him. Who controls us is determined by whether we submit to the Holy Spirit or submit to our soulish desires. These soulish desires emanate from our hearts and minds but often do become manifested in the flesh.

Sadly, some in Christianity have twisted Ephesians 5:18-19 as a license to practice the demonic doctrine of being "Drunk in the Spirit". You may have witnessed this spectacle when people begin stumbling on the stage or start slurring their words while blasphemously attributing this "spiritual drunkenness" to God. Many verses refute this evil teaching yet some circles embrace this false doctrine as Biblical.

In contrast, just like one can be filled with the Holy Spirit, Satan can also fill a believer's heart.

> *But Peter said, Ananias, why hath Satan filled thine heart to lie to the Holy Ghost, and to keep back part of the price of the land?* **(Acts 5:3)**

This verse shows that even a saved man can let himself be controlled by his carnal nature and be under the influence of Satan. Believers need to guard against this tragic occurrence.

Spirit Filling & Music

Returning to Ephesians 5:18, we are reminded about the critical role music and meditating on godly things plays in being filled with the Holy Spirit:

> And be not drunk with wine, wherein is excess; but be filled with the Spirit; (Eph 5:18) Speaking to yourselves in psalms and hymns and spiritual songs, singing and making melody in your heart to the Lord; (Eph 5:19)

God lovingly instructs that we should speak to ourselves in psalms, hymns and spiritual songs. (This author believes that this could mean either speaking to ourselves audibly or inaudibly.)

No doubt we are directed to use the Psalms because they were inspired lyrical compositions that contained truths and revelations about all three persons of the Godhead. The Psalms contain theology, doctrine, history and even unfulfilled prophecies which make them the most heavenly arrangements that a believer can sing.

This speaking or singing of the Psalms along with godly hymns and spiritual songs serves a couple of purposes. First, it is a form of meditating on God's truth, righteousness, love, law, mercy, future kingdom etc. Second, as we meditate/sing on these eternal precepts you begin to fill your heart and mind with

God's truths in a melodic way. As your heart and mind are filled with these songs of truths you can't help but memorize these Scriptures that are set to music. This musical and lyrical phenomenon forms one of the proofs that a believer is Holy Spirit filled. Not only is it one the proofs but it is also one of the pre-requisites of Spirit filling. Why, because you are filling your heart, mind and soul with godly words and sounds. In this manner you limit the opportunity for lustful sounds, thoughts, songs to enter into the temple of the Holy Spirit.

In most ways, what goes into our hearts and minds via our ears is more important than what we eat daily. As such, meditation and singing of psalms, hymns and spiritual songs is essential for abundant living. It is very sad that local churches have lost sight of this eternal truth. Many song leaders know very little about the power of music and lyrics (for good or for evil). This is one of the reasons why a significant number of churches have moved toward worldly music manipulation that provides an adrenaline surge but no filling…no melody making in your heart.

Anyone who has spent time in the world as an unbeliever is cognizant that advertisers, business people and even witches know a great deal about music's seductive and manipulative power. Woefully, many "worship leaders" willingly ignore the Biblical truth and the worldly evidences all under the pretext of being "relevant". These leaders are often deluded into believing that they are worshipping in spirit when in reality they are worshipping soulishly. In these cases, emotion is frequently confused as Spirit-filled. The great proof of this is seen when people experience church emotional highs but little change toward holiness.

Spirit Filling & Joy

The word for being "filled" (pleh-roh'-o) is linked with the word "joy" in twelve New Testament verses. This clearly indicates that one of the proofs of a Holy Spirit filled believer is a joyous heart. This joyous heart then leads to a joyous outlook that eventually leads to joyous behavior and words. The operative word is "joy-full". The following verses speak this lovely truth:

> Now the God of hope *fill you with all joy and peace* in believing, that ye may abound in hope, through the power of the Holy Ghost. **(Romans 15:13)**

> And these things write we unto you, *that your joy may be full*. **(1 John 1:4);**

> I would not write with paper and ink: but I trust to come unto you, and speak face to face, *that our joy may be full*. **(2 John 1:12)**

There is a significant connection between being Holy Spirit filled and the fruit of joy. This isn't surprising since Holy Spirit filling can be derived from filling your mind with things that are honest, just, pure, lovely and praiseworthy.

Only our obedience to God's commands allows the Holy Spirit freedom to work within us. Because we are sinners that still sin, it is impossible to be filled with the Holy Spirit all of the time. However, when we confess our sins to God, start living in obedience and begin living in His will, we will become filled with the Holy Spirit and filled with joy. This joyous filling becomes one of the evidences, as well as the blessings, that are bestowed upon us by our Omnipotent God!

CHAPTER TEN – IN WHICH NAME? & BAPTIZED FOR THE DEAD?

"How can we know God's Truths for living unless we allow His Sword to penetrate our shield of pride." (Dr. Luis C. Ruiz)

At this juncture in our journey, by God's grace, we have covered various critical elements on the doctrine of baptisms. Now we start delving into some unique or dare I say bizarre areas of Biblical study. Before moving ahead let's revisit a couple of verses with the purpose of steadfastly anchoring our minds.

> *For by one Spirit are we all baptized into one body, whether we be Jews or Gentiles, whether we be bond or free; and have been all made to drink into one Spirit.* (**1Cor 12:13**)

> *One Lord, one faith, one baptism,* (**Eph 4:5**)

These verses can help us navigate through much of the doctrinal confusion. They can also provide comfort when someone doubts their walk in Christ.

In this chapter, we will be covering two seemingly miscellaneous but still very important topics on water baptism. They are important topics because they create false worship and further divide the body of Christ.

Which Name?

The first topic deals with which name should we be water baptized in. Should we be water baptized "in the name of Jesus" or "in the name of the Father, the Son and the Holy Spirit"? As with all doctrinal dilemmas, let's review the main verses in question starting with Matthew 28:19.

> *Go ye therefore, and teach all nations, baptizing them in the name of the Father, and of the Son, and of the Holy Ghost:*

Here our Lord Jesus, after His resurrection, instructs His chosen Apostles on how they should water baptize believers in the soon to arrive church age. By extension, He is also instructing us as we build upon that foundation of the early church. Water baptism here is paralleled with discipleship not salvation. It is considered by many to be the first step of Christian discipleship. Hence, being water baptized of your own free will infers being a disciple of Christ. However, now our focus becomes that Jesus Christ Himself commanded that we should be baptized in the name of the Father, the Son and the Holy Spirit.

A seeming contradiction then emerges as we read of a pattern that surfaces throughout the early church specifically in the Book of Acts. Only in the book of Acts and nowhere else in the New Testament do we read about which name is used when water baptizing believers. The first account occurs in Acts 2:38.

> *Then Peter said unto them, Repent, and be* <u>*baptized every one of you in the name of Jesus Christ*</u> *for the remission of sins, and ye shall receive the gift of the Holy Ghost.*
> *(Acts 2:38)*

This of course occurred at Pentecost with the previously saved by faith but now soon-to-be Holy Spirit baptized Jewish believers. On to Acts 8:12:

> *But when they believed Philip preaching the things concerning the kingdom of God, and the name of Jesus Christ, they were baptized, both men and women. (Acts 8:12)...(For as yet he was fallen upon none of them: only they were baptized in the name of the Lord Jesus.) (Acts 8:16)*

As you recall, this water baptism occurred when the Gospel of the Messiah reached the Samaritans at Samaria. Moving to Acts 10:48:

> *And he commanded them to be baptized in the name of the Lord. Then prayed they him to tarry certain days.*

This event occurred when the Gospel of Jesus the Christ reached the Gentiles via the Apostles Peter and John. Now to Acts 19:5:

> *When they heard this, they were baptized in the name of the Lord Jesus. (Acts 19:5)*

This last event occurred with the already saved Jewish disciples that had only previously experienced the water baptism of John the Baptist.

The final verse is found in Acts 22:16 which reads:

> *And now why tarriest thou? arise, and be baptized, and wash away thy sins, calling on the name of the Lord.*

This verse is speaking of Saul (soon to be Paul) as a newborn believer while he was in Damascus.

Jesus' Command

Stepping back and reviewing the Bible's whole counsel on the matter, it is clear that the Lord Jesus commanded the Apostles to baptize in the name of the Father, the Son and the Holy Spirit. However, we then read of the five instances where the Apostles invoked the name of our Master in slightly different ways. They were: "Jesus Christ", "the Lord Jesus" (twice), in His "name" and "Lord".

Given the apparent contradictions, a few questions can be asked. First, were the Apostles disobedient to Christ in these instances? We know that the Apostles were at times disobedient (Acts 1 and Galatians 2) but it isn't conclusive in these cases.

A second question we can ask is, similar to being Holy Spirit baptized, is water baptism in the name of Jesus restricted only to the establishing of the church's early foundation? This possibility cannot be ruled out since the book of Acts depicts a transitional period (transitioning from the Mosaic Law to the Law of Christ) that lays the foundation of the church.

The third and final questions could be: do we have liberty to practice either one? Should we be dogmatic about one over the other?

Prior to resolving the alleged enigma, let's first establish the Biblical fact that names are important to God. Names are certainly important for salvation as Acts 2:21 and Romans 10:13 state that "whosoever calls on the name of the Lord (Jesus) shall be saved. Acts 4:12 likewise states:

for there is none other name under heaven given among men, whereby we must be saved. **(Acts 4:12)**

Further showing that names are important, in a sardonic way, God conveys that a Heavenly name is essential in water baptism in 1 Corinthians 13:13-15.

Is Christ divided? was Paul crucified for you? or were ye baptized in the name of Paul? **(1Cor 1:13)** *I thank God that I baptized none of you, but Crispus and Gaius;* **(1Cor 1:14)** *Lest any should say that I had baptized in mine own name.* **(1Cor 1:15)**

This passage unequivocally teaches that we cannot water baptize with a name that is not representative of the one true God!

Different Perspectives

Let's also briefly analyze three different and somewhat opposing viewpoints. Those who side with baptizing in the name of Jesus state that the Apostles set the precedent for the church since it occurred after Pentecost. They would state that there is no other name other than Jesus whereby man would be saved. They would also say that Jesus has been given all the power and authority.

One group which baptizes in the name of Jesus call themselves: Oneness Pentecostals, also known as the "Jesus Only" movement. This group sadly takes it to a blasphemous level not because they baptize in the name of the Lord Jesus but because they deny the Biblical differences between the Father, the Son and the

Holy Spirit. As well, they explicitly deny the personal characteristics and ministry of the Holy Spirit.

A second viewpoint holds onto the position that as long as the baptism was Biblically-based, the name used may not matter. Hence, they would accept the baptism as long as it was conducted as a...

- A public expression of one's salvation.

- A public demonstration of what occurred inside a person.

- Emanated from a desire of being identified as a disciple of Christ

- Complete immersion where the Trinity is not denied

For this camp, if all these points are satisfied it would be a Biblically acceptable position.

The third viewpoint, one many solid expositors side with is the position that baptizes in the name of the Father, the Son and the Holy Spirit. They (and the author) would state that Jesus' command would supersede any of the Apostles actions. This position would maintain that doctrine ideally should always be grounded on clear commands when provided for in God's Word (prescriptive rather than descriptive). When explicit directives or commands are not found then one may default to the example of Holy Spirit filled people in Scripture. This position would also hold that we should always incorporate the comprehensive approach that includes the Godhead (the Father, Son and Holy Spirit) since each Person is part of the salvation and sanctification. In addition, never was a Scriptural command given to baptize exclusively in the name of Jesus.

It is fascinating to note the subtle choice of words used in our Lord's command in Matthew 28:19.

> *Go ye therefore, and teach all nations, baptizing them in the name of the Father, and of the Son, and of the Holy Ghost:*

Notice that "name" and not "names" is used. This use of the Greek noun "onoma" subtly asserts the unity of the Godhead while emphasizing their distinctiveness.

In summation, this third position is the most Biblically viable since it was commanded by our Master, Lord Jesus. While He could have commanded anything, in Jesus' eternal humility, He instructed His followers to be baptized in the name of the everlasting Godhead. Hence, to truly worship in Spirit and in Truth we should submit to God the Son's humble example and directions.

For the Dead?

The next topic comes from a very cryptic verse that is used by some heretical groups to forward their false teachings. The verse is 1 Corinthians 15:29 and it states:

> *Else what shall they do which are baptized for the dead, if the dead rise not at all? why are they then baptized for the dead?*

A well-known expositor of the 1800's, Adam Clarke said of this verse,

> "This is certainly the most difficult verse in the NT; for, notwithstanding the greatest and wisest of men have laboured to explain it, there are to this day nearly as many

different interpretations of it as there are interpreters." (Adam Clarke's 1810/1825 Commentary and Critical Notes on the Bible. The Word Bible Software. 1 Corinthians 15:29)

As such, many odd and downright anti-Biblical conjectures have come from this verse. The Mormons have used it to teach that we should be baptized for dead loved ones. Roman Catholicism takes it a step further by stating that if you can be baptized for dead loved ones then you can pray for them to specifically get them out of purgatory. Both of these doctrines are what the Bible calls "damnable heresies". (2 Peter 2:1)

A second postulation states that the Holy Spirit is possibly presenting that some of the Corinthian believers were practicing the pagan ritual of proxy baptism for those who died unbaptized. This view is not supported by the context and Scripture in general. Each soul is held accountable by God for their actions or inactions. Hence, faith and works cannot be assigned.

Another premise asserts that martyrdom may have taken place against those who took a public stand for Christ especially at the time of their baptism. As the next group of believers stepped into the waters of baptism, in a figurative sense they were being baptized for, or in the place of the dead. Again, this supposition is not supported by the context and Scripture in general.

The Holy Spirit via the Apostle Paul clearly is not suggesting either one of these teachings as a Christian doctrine. An important axiom in Bible interpretation is that one should never build doctrine from a vague and difficult passage to interpret Scripture but rather it must have clear and collective support.

God's Complete Counsel

Holy Spirit filled interpreters suggest (the author agrees), that straightforward interpretations can be found when you take the **whole bible** as context. When practicing this approach, often the best interpretation is also the simplest. One such supporting passage is Romans 6:3-5.

> *Know ye not, that so many of us as were baptized into Jesus Christ were baptized into his death?* **(Romans 6:3)** *Therefore we are buried with him by baptism into death: that like as Christ was raised up from the dead by the glory of the Father, even so we also should walk in newness of life.* **(Romans 6:4)** *For if we have been planted together in the likeness of his death, we shall be also in the likeness of his resurrection:* **(Romans 6:5)**

Romans 6:3-5 states that the born-again are baptized into the death of Jesus Christ. The sense given is that we are baptized to symbolize Christ's death, burial and resurrection. When a disciple voluntarily gets immersed it becomes a symbol of death...the death of Christ. It also signifies death to the disciple's old life.

Likewise, when a disciple comes up out of the water it symbolizes resurrection unto eternal life. Thus, when 1 Corinthians 15:29 speaks of being baptized for the dead, it signifies that believers are trusting in the resurrection of Jesus. Why bother getting baptized in the name of Jesus if He didn't rise from the dead?

In the end, even with the Holy Spirit permanently dwelling inside of us as well as us possessing God's inspired and complete revelation, we still can only see heavenly things through dark tinted glass. On one hand, this should greatly humble us. On the other hand, it should also encourage us to search His Words daily to determine His desired will for our life.

> *The Lord is not slack concerning his promise, as some men count slackness; but is longsuffering to us-ward, not willing that **any** should perish, but that **all** should come to repentance.* **(2 Peter 3:9)**

CHAPTER ELEVEN – WATER BAPTISMAL REGENERATION

"The eternal Words of Jesus are life giving. Let's stop trying to wring the life out of them with our own opinions and feelings!"
(Dr. Luis C. Ruiz)

Continuing our study on the doctrine of baptisms, in this chapter we'll focus on a teaching that states that though you believe that Jesus is God; that He died for your sins and rose from the dead and even professed it with your mouth you still may not go to heaven.

It is a teaching that believes that the work of water baptism is necessary to realizing eternal salvation. It basically is a form of Lordship Salvation because it requires an individual to do certain works or avoid certain sins in order to get into heaven. A couple of verses are used to further this position. The first one we'll address starts at Mark 16:15.

> *And he said unto them, Go ye into all the world, and preach the gospel to every creature. (Mark 16:15) He that believeth and is baptized shall be saved; but he that believeth not shall be damned. (Mark 16:16) And these signs shall follow them that believe; In my name shall they cast out devils; they shall speak with new tongues; (Mark 16:17) They shall take up serpents; and if they drink any deadly thing, it shall not hurt them; they shall lay hands on the sick, and they shall recover. (Mark 16:18)*

Some use Mark 16:16 to prove the necessity of water baptism for salvation. However, by comparing Scripture with Scripture, we know that it is faith that saves while water baptism is the symbol and evidence of one's faith. A careful reading of Mark 16:16 confirms this truth.

Notice that it does not say that those who are not baptized shall be damned; it simply says those who do not believe will be damned. Remember Acts 16 when the Philippian jailer asked, *"...What must I do to be saved?"* The Holy Spirit via the Apostle Paul simply replied, *"Believe on the Lord Jesus Christ, and thou shalt be saved..."* (Acts 16:30-31). After the jailer believed on Christ, he was baptized that same night. Thus, the water baptism was a product of his salvation not the opposite. By contrast, we previously covered that Holy Spirit Baptism is the mark and seal of adoption that accompanies salvation (Galatians 4:6; Ephesians 1:11-12).

Another confirmation comes from the Apostle Paul's telling statement: *"For Christ sent me not to baptize, but to preach the gospel."* (1 Cor. 1:17). Leaving souls unsaved (by supposedly not water baptizing them) indeed would have been tragic words from a man who spent many years reaching thousands with the Good News of Jesus Christ. He even desired to be accursed in order for the Jewish elect to believe in Christ. Therefore, he would not have walked away from thousands that were still going to hell.

That said we must not forget that water baptism is indeed critical for obedience to God and the spiritual growth of the believer. However, as proven earlier, water baptism exclusively follows salvation in the church age and should be one of the first steps of obedience after salvation!

Our Lord's Audience

Another major point about the Mark 16 passage often missed is that in context our Lord is communicating directly to the chosen Apostles. This becomes evident especially when one considers that Jesus speaks of His disciples not being killed by snakes or poison, speaking in new languages and casting out of devils. This again is pivotal when one keeps to the truth that the Apostles laid the foundation of the church. Therefore, Christ isn't broadly addressing anyone (especially Gentiles) and isn't addressing future church generations. So while Mark 16:16 was written for our learning it was directly written to the chosen Apostles.

The Ark and the Flood

Another passage often brought up in water baptismal regeneration is 1 Peter 3:20-21.

> *Which sometime were disobedient, when once the longsuffering of God waited in the days of Noah, while the ark was a preparing, wherein few, that is, eight souls were saved by water. The like figure whereunto even baptism doth also now save us (not the putting away of the filth of the flesh, but the answer of a good conscience toward God,) by the resurrection of Jesus Christ:*

To properly understand this passage, we must see the ark metaphorically as a picture of the Lord Jesus; a symbol of the only way of salvation. The global

113

water flood depicted the judgment of God. When the flood came, only those who were inside the ark were saved; all those on the ou+tside perished.

The ark had waters of judgment beneath it, on top of it, and all around it but still safely carried the believing eight occupants through the storm into a renewed creation. Likewise, Christ is the only way of salvation; those who are in Christ are saved. Those on the outside are lost. He will carry His redeemed through the storms and eventually into a renewed earth!

To clarify, the water was not the means of salvation; the ark was the place of refuge. The ark went through the waters of judgment; it took the full impact of the storm. In the same way, Christ bore the fury of God's judgment against our sins. For those who are in Him there is no judgment (John 5:24). So here, water baptism means judgment.

We must keep to memory that the baptism associated with salvation is Holy Spirit baptism which occurs when the Holy Spirit lives inside of the new believer. Hence, 1 Peter 3 is really saying that just as Noah and his family had to willingly enter the ark to be saved, we likewise have to believe (of our own accord) that Jesus is our Savior. In effect, it is a reverse typology meaning that it represents the opposite of what baptismal regeneration proponents advocate.

The Two Baptisms of Jesus

A deeper exegesis pulls into our consideration the two baptisms of our Lord Jesus. The first baptism occurred at the Jordan River with John the Baptist and was a water baptism. The second baptism involved His soul and took place during His suffering and death commencing in Gethsemane and culminating at Golgotha (Calvary).

> *But I have a baptism to be baptized with; and how am I straitened* (anguished) *till it be accomplished!* **Luke 12:50** (emphasis added)

This verse as well as parallel verses in Matthew 23:20 and Mark 10:39 speak of the baptism; the immersion; the complete inundating of God's wrath on the sin of the world that Jesus the Christ had to suffer and endure. Contextually, this is the wrath spoken of in 1 Peter 3:21!

In addition, let's not forget what our Lord told the penitent malefactor who was crucified at his side:

> *Verily I say unto thee, To day shalt thou be with me in paradise.* **(Luke 23:43)**

By this we know that for his faith the crucified sinner was pardoned, and went with Christ to paradise and eventually to the third heaven.

Born of Water

A final verse that is often used as a proof-text to promote water baptismal regeneration is John 3:5.

> *Jesus answered, Verily, verily, I say unto thee, Except a man be born of water and of the Spirit, he cannot enter into the kingdom of God.* **(John 3:5)**

A close examination shows that this verse speaks of being born of water...a physical birth. Our Lord Jesus could have easily used the word for baptism to indicate otherwise. Being born of water was a Jewish expression meaning "physical birth." This verse also has in view the incorrect notion held by some Jews that being a Jew by birth was sufficient to enter the kingdom of God. To further cement the point, in John 3:6, Jesus clearly delineates the physical from the spiritual:

That which is born of the flesh is flesh; and that which is born of the Spirit is spirit.

So while the spiritual new birth is signified and represented by water baptism, Scripture repeatedly teaches that immersion is not the agent of salvation.

Water Baptism's Purpose

In concluding this chapter, let's review the Biblical purpose and significance of water baptism:

- It is a public act of faith.
- It is an act of openly identifying yourself with Christ.
- It is an act of obedience.
- It is a figure, a picture...a symbol of salvation.
- It identifies the believer with Christ's death, burial and resurrection.
- It symbolizes the Christian's union with Christ!
- It is a proclamation that he or she is a new creation in Jesus.
- It is a crucial aspect of growth in Christ!

When a disciple of Christ fully and properly examines all of the verses in question, the Bible overwhelmingly states that salvation is by faith alone!

For God so loved the world, that he gave his only begotten Son, that whosoever believeth in him should not perish, but have everlasting life. (John 3:16)

Not by works of righteousness which we have done, but according to his mercy he saved us, by the washing of regeneration, and renewing of the Holy Ghost; (Titus 3:5)

For by grace are ye saved through faith; and that not of yourselves: it is the gift of God: (Eph 2:8) Not of works, lest any man should boast. (Eph 2:9)

CHAPTER TWELVE – INFANT SPRINKLING & "COVENANT BAPTISM"

"There are numerous traditions and voices that teach as many divergent and contradictory doctrines. Will you follow one of them or the source...the Bible?" (Dr. Luis C. Ruiz)

So far throughout the treatise we have been able to establish what water and Holy Spirit baptism truly means for us during the church age. We have evidenced a Biblical standard on how to worship God in spirit and in truth while also refuting false doctrine found across the Christian landscape. In this chapter, we address another of those errant teachings.

"Covenant Baptism"

This teaching states that within the church, infant baptism has replaced the Jewish covenant of circumcision. Using catchphrase marketing, some have called it: "Covenant Baptism". Largely unbeknownst to many in this camp is that they have embraced the Roman Catholic doctrine of Infant Baptism while attempting to justify it by Scripture twisting to suit their denominational creeds.

In addressing this doctrinal matter, we have to remember that most of the reformers were Roman Catholics that were not looking to leave the Vatican but rather reform it. We also have to remember that true churches have always existed outside of Rome since the establishment of the church at Pentecost. Long before the reformers, groups like the Albigenses, the

Waldensians, the Paulicians, the Lollards etc. kept to sounder Biblical teachings that countered the Rome and Constantinople religious power structures. This is the reason why they were ruthlessly persecuted by the Vatican for hundreds of years. By God's grace, the Gates of Hell did not prevail against these true Christians and we should not forget their sacrifice.

The 21st century church is also eternally indebted to the protestant reformers for standing-up to Rome and bringing to light several heretical dogmas with the most egregious being works-based salvation. While this feat was commendable, sadly they fell way short of complete reformation. As a result, many Reformed and Mainline churches adopted a litany of sordid Vatican doctrines. Along with embracing infant baptism (sometimes as a sacrament), many also adopted Romanism's end-times position of amillennial eschatology. The reformed church also embraced certain aspects of Vatican church government (hierarchical ecclesiology) along with the replacement of Israel with the church. Often called New or Spiritual Israel, "Replacement Theology" enabled the holding of a distorted view of election.

In order to justify "covenant baptism", one has to ignore multiple passages that clearly teach that baptism is for someone that has believed and professed that Jesus is their Messiah and that they want to be publicly immersed. One also has to ignore the early church witness that only immersed consenting believers in baptismal pools found in churches for hundreds of years.

Circumcision to Baptism?

Let's now add the element of circumcision to our examination as we turn to Colossians 2:11-13.

> *In whom also ye are circumcised with the circumcision made without hands, in putting off the body of the sins of the flesh by the circumcision of Christ:* **(Col 2:11)** *Buried with him in baptism, wherein also ye are risen with him through the faith of the operation of God, who hath raised him from the dead.* **(Col 2:12)** *And you, being dead in your sins and the uncircumcision of your flesh, hath he quickened together with him, having forgiven you all trespasses;* **(Col 2:13)**

Physical circumcision was a commandment/law in Judaism. It was a procedure in which a knife was applied to the foreskin of an eight day old male. To the Jew, it was a sign that indicated obedience to God...of being separated to Him. At the same time, this separated the Jew from the Pagan, Gentile world and its evil practices. The sign of circumcision was mandatory for the Jewish male and is mentioned in well over 110 verses throughout both the Old and New Testaments.

The New Testament also describes the Jews as those of the circumcision and designates the Gentiles as the uncircumcised. Any male born within Israel or within their camp had to be circumcised - Jewish or not. All foreigners or strangers or aliens within Israel had to obey all 613 Mosaic statutes and therefore had to be circumcised.

Another important point is that while the Bible mostly speaks about physical circumcision of the Jewish male (by birth or by conversion) it also speaks about being spiritually circumcised in the heart. Ezekiel 44:9 actually mentions both a physical and a spiritual circumcision.

> *Thus saith the Lord GOD; No stranger, uncircumcised in heart, nor uncircumcised in flesh, shall enter into my sanctuary, of any stranger that is among the children of Israel.*

The Bible also presents a vehement debate throughout the Book of Acts (especially chapter 15) as to whether Gentiles should be circumcised after believing in Jesus as Christ. The Holy Spirit's response to this matter is given in Romans, 1 Corinthians and Galatians. In summary, the guidance was that Gentiles were not obligated to circumcise their male infants but rather had the liberty to or not circumcise.

Thus, in Colossians 2:11, physical circumcision is not in view, but rather that spiritual circumcision which is true of everyone who has put their faith and trust in the Lord Jesus. This is clear from the expression *"the circumcision made without hands"*. What the verse is actually teaching is that every believer is circumcised in the heart by the supernatural circumcision of Christ.

In other words, when a person is saved, he becomes associated with Christ, and renounces any hope of earning or deserving salvation through their so-called good works. Thus, the sins of the flesh have been forgiven through the spiritual circumcision of Christ. Through Christ's circumcision of the heart, those that freely believe in Him are eternally saved and justified.

In verse 12, the subject changes from circumcision to that of baptism. Just as circumcision speaks of death to the flesh, baptism speaks of the burial of the old man. In tandem, this is teaching that believers have not only died with Christ, but have been buried with Him. This is because both spiritual circumcision and Spirit Baptism takes place at the time of conversion with the only outward expression occurring in the waters of baptism. In this context, water Baptism speaks of the burial of the "old man". Not only have we been crucified with Christ and buried with Him but we have also risen with Him to walk in newness of life. All of this takes place at the time of conversion. It occurs through a believer's faith and through the working of God.

In verse 13 we're told that every person, though being dead in trespasses and the uncircumcision of their flesh, is instantly made alive, together with Christ, at the moment of justification through faith. Beautifully, believers will not be damned for their trespasses since God Himself has forgiven them all.

What is Circumcision?

At this juncture, inserting two main points about circumcision are needful:

1. Circumcision was a sign of the Abrahamic covenant with only his male physical seed. As such, the covenant of blood was only required of the men not the women.

2. Nowhere in the Bible do we learn that "baptism replaces circumcision". In the Colossian epistle, it is merely stated that when one becomes a Christian they are *"circumcised with the circumcision made without hands, by putting off the body of the sins of the flesh"* (Colossians 2:11).

All born-again believers in Colossae were old enough to understand what it meant to "cut off the body of the sins of the flesh" at their conversion. Beautiful, precious babies who are "christened" have no knowledge of sin and no knowledge of God. So in reality, babies were actually excluded, not included, in this passage.

Spiritual Dangers

It is also paramount to present several Biblical reasons why it is dangerous to teach that "infant baptism replaced circumcision":

- "Sprinkled babies" eventually grow-up and feel a false sense that they are obeying God since they were baptized into the "faith". (This author can personally attest to this fact.)

- Parents of "unsprinkled babies" can embrace a false sense of eternal insecurity if their infant sadly passes away.

- When babies are sprinkled there is no picture of the death, burial and resurrection of Christ.

- Infants provide no personal testimony.

- Circumcision was confined to males; baptism is for both male and female (cf. Galatians 3:28).

- If baptism were truly the antitype of circumcision, then only male children should be baptized at exactly 8 days of age.

- "The covenant of circumcision" (Acts 7:8) was confined to the <u>physical</u> descendants of Abraham, Isaac, and Jacob, and those converted to Judaism (Genesis 17:12-13; Exodus 12:48).

- Water baptism is for all nations (Matthew 28:19-20).

- Baptism shows the faith and obedience of the one being baptized.

- Circumcision shows the faith and obedience of the parents of the one being circumcised.

In addition, we must address the couple verses that speak of the "household being baptized' that are used to support infant baptism. This argument states that there had to be babies in those houses. One such verse points to the household Lydia being water baptized in Acts 16:15:

"And when she was baptized, and her household".

Errant teachers will contend that since the household was baptized there had to be infants present. This is clearly eisegesis or reading one's theological bias into the passage since the Bible is silent about babies being present. Nowhere in Scripture are infants mentioned in this respect!

The main point being that if we want to truly please God and truly obedient to Him, then water baptism must be a public demonstration of your faith. As the Bible decrees, it is a symbol of you identifying with your Saviour's death, burial and resurrection.

When we (the body of Christ) are obedient in these matters, we will bring blessings upon ourselves (temporal and eternal) and will bless others around us. Most importantly, we will bring glory to God through our faith and obedience.

CHAPTER THIRTEEN – OTHER IMPORTANT ASPECTS

"To right divide the Word of Truth means to mark the exact cuts required by the Word, separated by the precise distances needed by the Word only after measuring multiple times!" (Dr. Luis C. Ruiz)

This chapter addresses several miscellaneous water baptism questions and issues. While these areas may not be classified by some as the most "weightier matters" of water baptism they still represent areas that can impact the growth of the disciple as well as the discipler. As such, it is worthy to briefly address these subjects.

Who is Qualified to Baptize?

A topic of ecclesiological concern that occasionally surfaces is the subject of who is Biblically qualified to water baptize a believer. Analyzing Scripture, we identify a relative short list of the men who baptized others. They are:

1. John the Baptist
2. The Disciples of our Lord Jesus baptized during His earthly ministry (John 4:1-2)
3. The Disciples at Pentecost (Likely only the eleven Apostles plus Matthias baptized)
4. Phillip the Deacon baptizing the Samaritans
5. Ananias baptizing Saul (Acts 9:18)
6. The Apostle Peter with the Gentiles

7. The Apostle Paul (maybe Silas)

This baptizer list consists of five specific names (six of you include the possibility of Silas). One could then add the names of remaining eleven Apostles that walked with Jesus (Peter being previously included and likely including Judas) as well as Matthias. This brings the total of men that conducted water baptism observances in Scripture to a minimum of seventeen.

We can categorize the seventeen men that baptized others in the following manner.

- One was the forerunner of Jesus that came in the spirit of the prophet Elijah – John the Baptist.
- The God-ordained thirteen Apostles – This includes the original twelve along with Paul. Not all were saved by faith (Judas).
- The man-ordained Matthias.
- Phillip the Deacon
- The godly Silas
- The godly Ananias
- Of the above men, only Peter and John were self-identified as Elder/Pastors.
- Of these seventeen, fourteen were Apostles, one was a Deacon, two were Elders and two were humble ministers of God.

So while God did not expressly outline the qualifications of who was eligible to baptize, several conclusions could be drawn from this list. First, not all had official titles like Apostle and Deacons. Second, not all were pastor/elders. Third, all were men. Thus, there appears to be some Biblical flexibility as to who can baptize from a title perspective.

While this author highly urges that believers get water baptized by a Pastor/Elder of a Bible believing church, the flexibility offered by Scripture can be useful under certain extenuating circumstances. Some of these conditions include: Missionaries in their deployed country, travelling evangelists where no Bible churches are near and newly converted souls that soon may be dying. Some churches also have ordained deacons (similar to Philip) that perform baptisms.

Are all Water Baptisms Valid?

The next topic addressed is whether all water baptisms performed are valid. While the answer to this broad question can vary, here a few aspects to prayerfully consider; The most obvious water baptism that can be acknowledged as invalid is the one received by an individual that recognizes they were not born-again at the time of their immersion. Many of these situations come from individuals that were baptized at a younger age thinking that they were saved. Later in life, they truly came to faith and were publically re-baptized as a powerful testimony.

Another situation that could lead to consider re-baptism includes if someone was initially baptized in the name of Jesus and then desired to be immersed in the name of the Father, Son and the Holy Spirit. A re-baptism can also occur when it involves someone that was baptized believing that it was a salvific act. This believer will then want to get baptized with a Biblically correct heart motive.

Another instance where a believer could consider re-baptism is when they were first baptized by someone or a church that was later understood to be unbiblical.

In these cases, the Bible doesn't necessarily invalidate the previous baptism if done post-salvation and as a public testimony. On occasion, some of these believers come under conviction to get re-baptized in their new church. As a matter of liberty in Christ, the Bible does not prohibit this practice of re-baptizing.

Is Water Baptism for the Church?

The next topic to be deliberated is whether immersion is for the church age. This is a rather deep and multi-layered exposition and requires significant Bible study and prayer. The subject delves into the matter of whether the water baptism ordinance given by Jesus Christ ceased once the Gospel of the kingdom offer to the Jewish nation was temporarily rescinded. It is frequently a position advanced by scholars that hold to Hyper or Ultra Dispensational theology. (Subsequently called UD.)

The main driver of this doctrinal perspective is that there is a different covenant or dispensation that commences after either Acts 15 or 28. The reasons for their justification are as follows: first, the book of Acts is wholly or mostly transitional and not to be relied upon for establishing doctrine. Second, they hold that the complete revealing of the mystery of the church does not take place at Acts 2 but rather Acts 15 or 28. Third, and by extension, only the letters of Paul are worthy for doctrinal consumption. They contend that all other epistles were chronologically written before their perceived start of the church or apply only to a post-church rapture.

Therefore, as a result of the above interpretations, UDs broadly hold the view that water baptism is not commanded or practiced after the Acts chapters. They believe that any commands to water baptize occurred while the young church was still in its mystery form for the Gentiles. As such, they posit that water baptism should not be practiced throughout this portion of the church age.

It should be noted that there is some merit in the diligence exhibited by Ultra or Hyper Dispensational expositors. Their interpretation that the book of Acts is a transitional book (sparingly used for doctrine) as well as that the Law of Moses passed in 70 AD are well founded. They also embrace the Biblically accurate position that Israel and the church are distinct. For these and other reasons much of their theological work is deep and thought provoking.

That stated, there are several areas of interpretational and doctrinal concern. First, this camp tends to overly divide the Word. This creates exegetical difficulties when determining the start of the church and what ordinances it should adopt. As a corollary, their position that the church (ecclesia) has different meanings depending on when it is mentioned throughout Acts and the Epistles is eisegetical.

Second, it is problematic to claim that Jesus' command to go into, teach and baptize all nations does not apply to the church age. (It is even more problematic to assert that Jesus was only referring to Spirit baptism and not water baptism.) To hold this view, you would have to believe that Jesus' directive to baptize applied only to the Jewish portion of the nascent church for only a scant few years.

Third, the UD reliance on the dating of New Testament Epistles is really an exercise in eisegesis and extra-Biblical conjecture. One cannot date with certainty the letters that mention baptism (Romans, First Corinthians, Colossians, Hebrews and First Peter) to coincide with the official end of the Mosaic/Temple Age. Even if they were all dated prior to AD 70 (which is also an extra-Biblical date) you would then be left with only a sparse few epistles to establish church doctrine.

Fourth, stating that only the writings of the Apostle Paul have doctrinal authority have no clear Biblical validity. The Apostle Paul himself wrote that the church is built upon the "Apostles" plural and not merely him (Ephesians 2:20). He also wrote that the mysteries were "revealed unto his holy apostles and prophets" (Ephesians 3:5) and not him only.

As such, the UD doctrine of water baptism not being applicable to the church becomes untenable given the number of interpretations that are not firmly rooted in Scripture. Of concern is that the extra divisions or dispensations tend to unnecessarily splinter the body of Christ. However, what makes this doctrine most spiritually dangerous is that it completely negates the ordinance of a believer providing a public testimony of their saving faith. Sadly, also negated are the blessings of obedience.

What is a Church Ordinance?

At this point, a brief parenthetical study of the meaning of the term "church ordinance" is warranted. The word "ordinance(s)" is found 55 times in Scripture. The 46 mentions in the Old Testament mostly speak of Mosaic Law decrees, feasts and statutes as well as

God's ordered creation. In these instances, the verses always carry the sense of God's "rule of law" and His "orderly rituals".

Of the New Testament mentions, the verse most pertinent to our thesis is found in 1 Corinthians 11:2.

Now I praise you, brethren, that ye remember me in all things, and keep the ordinances, as I delivered them to you.

Here we read that the local church is to observe and practice the ordinances delivered unto them by the Apostle Paul. From this verse, a simple definition of church ordinance is that it is a prescriptive instruction that is adhered to by the local body of believers. Unquestionably, an ordinance in Scripture is God setting the proper order of service and worship for His people.

Delving deeper, an ordinance should possess three characteristics given by order of importance. First, it must be specifically directed by the Messiah or His chosen Apostles. Second, it must be observed by the early church. Third, it is described theologically in the epistles to the churches.

Let's analyze Biblical water baptism in light of the three above characteristics and establish that it is an ordinance throughout the church age. The first and most important point is plainly satisfied as Jesus our Messiah commanded all nations be water baptized (Matt. 28:18-20). The second facet is clearly fulfilled as the public water immersion of believers was extensively practiced by the Apostolic church (Acts 2:38, 41; 8:12-13, 36-38; 9:18; 10:47-48; 16:15, 33; 18:8; 19:5). Of significance, the newly saved Gentiles were also water baptized (Acts 10:47-48). The third point is also satisfied as water baptism was theologically explained in Romans 6:3-4 and Colossians 2:11-12.

> *Know ye not, that so many of us as were baptized into Jesus Christ were baptized into his death? (Romans 6:3) Therefore we are buried with him by baptism into death: that like as Christ was raised up from the dead by the glory of the Father, even so we also should walk in newness of life. (Romans 6:4)*

> *In whom also ye are circumcised with the circumcision made without hands, in putting off the body of the sins of the flesh by the circumcision of Christ: (Col 2:11) Buried with him in baptism, wherein also ye are risen with him through the faith of the operation of God, who hath raised him from the dead. (Col 2:12)*

A couple of crucial items can be extracted from the above verses. When a believer submits to water baptism, the immersion depicts our Master's burial. In essence, the Christian is identifying with Christ's death. The believer's coming up out of the water represents Jesus' glorious resurrection and God's power over death. Finally, just like Jesus received His glorified body after the resurrection, His disciples can likewise boldly "walk in newness of life" after their public proclamation. So while water baptism doesn't save eternally, it does provide the believer the added strength that comes from walking in obedience!

"Cleansing" or "Washing"

Another baptismal topic to be briefly assessed emanates from Ephesians 5:26:

That he might sanctify and cleanse it with the washing of water by the word

This seldom exposited verse is nestled within a section of Scripture that is either joyfully recited in marriage ceremonies or reticently repeated in marriage counseling. While it isn't technically a verse on baptism, it is often confused as one given its seemingly unique context.

At its center, expositors widely agree that the verse depicts the works of our Master Jesus with His bride: the church. This becomes apparent when verse 26 is read within its adjacent context.

Husbands, love your wives, even as Christ also loved the church, and gave himself for it; (Eph 5:25) That he might sanctify and cleanse it with the washing of water by the word, (Eph 5:26) That he might present it to himself a glorious church, not having spot, or wrinkle, or any such thing; but that it should be holy and without blemish. (Eph 5:27)

The remaining question for our purposes then is: what does it mean to *"sanctify and cleanse the church with the washing of water by the word"*? Plainly, the Eternal Word (which can mean Jesus Christ and/or His precious Words) is the agent that cleanses and sanctifies the body of Christ. It is the only way the church can be purged of any spot, wrinkle or blemish. Hence, water in this verse metaphorically represents the Word. Just like water physically cleanses, the Word "cleanses" the spirit by sanctifying it at conversion and "cleanses" the soul by sanctifying it by the growing in grace and knowledge of our Saviour.

Likewise in John 17:17, the Lord Jesus' prayer linked sanctification with His word:

"Sanctify them through thy truth: thy word is truth."

The Word of God, along with the convicting work of the Holy Spirit, cleanses us continually from the defilement and corrosiveness of sin.

Once all of the imperfections are miraculously removed, Jesus will then present the purified and holy church to Himself. He becomes both the presenter and the receiver. This isn't surprising since He is the Alpha and the Omega. What a wonderful picture of our God!

Similar to Ephesians 5:26, Titus 3:5 presents us with the lovely truth that we are eternally saved by the *"washing of regeneration"*. Here "washing" symbolically illustrates how we are cleansed when we are baptized (immersed) by the Holy Spirit. There are some that erroneously interpret "washing" to mean salvation via water baptism (adult or infant). However, the context is clear that figurative language is not used to denote actual water baptism but rather a spiritual and positional truth.

How Many Dunks?

The final topic to be addressed is a more light-hearted theme that deals with how many times should the baptized person be immersed? Not widely practiced, there are groups of churches that have embraced the practice of dunking people three times as a reverential testimony to all three persons of the Godhead. Their point is that they immerse three times because Jesus Christ commanded the church to baptize in the name of all three.

From a Biblical perspective there appears to be liberty in Christ to conduct thrice immersion. However, there are elements that are concerning. First, nowhere in Scripture do we read of someone being submerged more than once. Second, nowhere are we commanded to immerse multiple times.

While dunking three times may present a lovely picture of the Trinity some will invariably confuse Christian liberty with Christian doctrine. These lines often get blurred with newer or weaker believers. As such, it is always advisable to stay as close as possible to Scripture given man's propensity for error and our rapidity to fall away from pleasing God. The next chapter is to help us avoid this problem.

CHAPTER FOURTEEN – BIBLICAL BAPTISM & EXEGESIS

"We must never allow feelings and emotions to control how we live...even the ungodly know this simple truth." (Dr. Luis C. Ruiz)

In this final chapter, some recommendations that will help our interpretational approach with difficult to understand passages will be offered. The desired outcome being that we continue to grow in our understanding of Scripture that hopefully leads us to serve and worship God in the manner He decrees.

These pointers are not exhaustive or necessarily in order of importance or sequence. They are:

- Ask God for wisdom and understanding.
  - We are not God so it is imperative that we seek God's wisdom first and foremost.

- Humble yourself to the passage.
  - These are God's eternal Words of Life and Truth. We can't just treat them like we are reading a mere textbook. We should humbly submit to them.

- Read the passage multiple times....meditate on it.
  - Even after praying, there is still no substitute for re-reading the passage 5 to 10 times. Meditating on it is indispensable.

- Read the **whole** Bible.
  - Many have Biblical opinions but have never entirely read the Bible. (This author was one of those people.)

- Read in plain, common sense language:
  o Literal when literal, figurative when figurative, parable when parable, prophetic when prophetic etc.
- Conduct word studies of all of the words of passage...even the so-called unimportant words.
  o This is possibly one of the approaches that has helped this author the most.
- Understand the context (also called discourse analysis).
  o Biblical context "telescopes" from the immediate verses, to the chapter, to the book, to the whole Bible and back.
  o This approach ties into multiple reads of the passage and the complete 66 books of the Bible.
- Set aside emotional bias.
  o This is one of the most problematic areas toward attaining God's truth.
  o Too many are wed to what their first pastor or favorite author taught them.
  o It can also be driven by emotional ties to the teachings of loved ones or the person that led them to Christ.
- Set aside denominational and theological bias.
  o Leaders are often trained within a theological framework that has shackled them from being led by the Spirit of Truth.
  o Some pastors come to believe the Bible more than their denominational doctrine but say and do nothing because they are receiving a paycheck.

- Know to whom the passage was written. While all Scripture is profitable to you, most Scripture was not written to you.
    o Groups often directly spoken to include: Israelites under the Law of Moses, Chosen Apostles, Born-Again Jews, Born-Again Gentiles.
- Know that some commands have been superseded by a newer commands and covenants (some refer to them as dispensations). This is called God's Progressive Revelation!
- Always search to interpret the passage prior to searching for the practical application (what it means to me).
    o Why? Because you will never know what it means to you if you don't know its true interpretation.
    o Searching for a practical application before understanding the interpretation is an all too frequent phenomena with "cell groups", small study groups. And even Sunday sermons.
- Embrace God's whole counsel and not man-made philosophies, writings and theological frameworks.
    o Man-made theories often ignore multiple verses to preserve their "cherished doctrines".
    o This includes: TULIP, Papal Decrees, Arminianism, Ellen G White, Ecumenical Creeds and Councils, Charismaticism etc.)
- Seek godly teachers. The New Testament gave us many examples. Some are:
    o Jesus instructed the Apostles both as a man and after His ascension.

- o Peter, John, Jacob (James) instructed many.
- o Paul had human instruction via Barnabas, Peter, James etc.
- o Peter had human instruction via Paul.
- o Barnabas had human instruction via Paul.
- o Seeking Godly teachers is vital as you can learn different things from different people. Even then, everything has to be tested against Scripture.
- o Only the Bible determines if you disagree. Please don't disagree because of your feelings or your cherished tradition or your favored philosophical view.

- For your main study select a Bible that is an accurate and faithful translation of a superior set of Hebrew, Aramaic and Greek texts. This author utilizes the KJV in English.
  - o The translation must come from a reliable text that is derived from a preserved manuscript.
  - o Some "Bibles" are really paraphrases and sometimes nothing more than a commentary. They can be confusing and at times spiritually dangerous.
  - o From what version are you getting your main Biblical meal/instruction?
  - o On the other hand, reading multiple Bibles can help deepen comprehension. (This author often reads Scripture in Spanish to augment.)

- Read multiple and varied commentaries.
  - o While one should mostly use trusted expositors mature believers can find value in diverse commentaries.

- o This may be confusing at first but with the help of the Holy Spirit, your knowledge will expand and be more anchored. In time, you will be able to aptly and quickly identify heresy.
- Do not rely on commentaries
  - o To their detriment, many get enamored with commentaries that agree with their views. This is often the case with those that embrace creeds and historical precedents.

By way of example, let's apply some of these elements to our study on the doctrine of baptisms.

- Conduct a word study on the words: baptism, baptize and baptized. (These verses are provided in the appendix.)

- Understand that the English word "baptism" is a transliteration of the Greek word. A true translation would be immerse or completely surrounded.

- Be clear whether the Bible is referring to baptism of the Holy Spirit or by water. Let the context drive the meaning!

- Understand who was experiencing the Spirit or Water baptism and when it was occurring.

- Understand the distinction between "faith" and "good works".

- Understand the difference between "works" and "fruit".

- Understand that water baptism is a work of obedience. Water baptism isn't a fruit and is not equivalent to faith.

- Be clear whether the word "save" or "saved" is referring to "being saved from eternal hell" or "being saved from an earthly calamity".
  - o Let the context drive the meaning.
  - o The Greek word "sozo" can mean either eternal or temporal salvation.

Most importantly, we should seek to humble ourselves before our Mighty God and Creator. We should draw nigh to Him. We should lean on His understanding. We should rest in His gentle yoke. We should ask for forgiveness as we confess our sins to Him. We should perpetually thank Him for His mercy and goodness...which lasts forever. And finally, we can pray for Him to rapture His church and eventually return to establish His literal kingdom here on earth.

> *He which testifieth these things saith, Surely I come quickly. Amen. Even so, come, Lord Jesus.* **(Rev 22:20)**

SCRIPTURE CITATIONS

Genesis 2:7
Genesis 17:12-13
Exodus 12:48
Proverbs 14:12
Isaiah 40:3-5
Isaiah 53:7-8
Ezekiel 44:9
Malachi 3:1
Matthew 3:5-13
Matthew 3:8
Matthew 3:10
Matthew 3:13-16
Matthew 3:15
Matthew 4:4
Matthew 5:19
Matthew 9:17
Matthew 11:13
Matthew 13:24-30
Matthew 13:36-43
Matthew 23:20
Matthew 28:18-20
Matthew 29:19
Mark 2:22
Mark 10:39
Mark 16:15
Mark 16:15-18
Mark 16:16
Mark 16:17
Luke 3:3
Luke 3:16
Luke 3:16-17
Luke 11:17

Luke 11:38
Luke 12:50
Luke 16:16
Luke 16:31
Luke 23:43
Luke 24:49
John 1:12
John 3:5
John 3:6
John 3:16
John 4:12
John 4:23-24
John 4:39-42
John 5:24
John 5:46
John 5:47
John 17:17
John 20:21-23
John 20:22
Acts 1:4-8
Acts 1:4-5
Acts 1:5
Acts 2:1-4
Acts 2:21
Acts 2:37-44
Acts 2:38
Acts 2:41
Acts 4:1-2
Acts 4:8
Acts 4:12
Acts 5:3
Acts 6:3

Acts 6:5	Romans 3:21-30
Acts 7:8	Romans 4:5
Acts 7:55	Romans 6:3-4
Acts 8:1	Romans 6:3-5
Acts 8:12	Romans 10:9-10
Acts 8:13	Romans 10:13
Acts 8:12-17	Romans 11:25
Acts 8:14-17	Romans 15:13
Acts 8:16	Romans 16:17
Acts 8:26	Romans 16:25
Acts 8:27-28	1 Corinthians 1:14-17
Acts 8:29-30	1 Corinthians 1:17
Acts 8:31-35	1 Corinthians 3:10
Acts 8:36-37	1 Corinthians 3:12-15
Acts 8:36-38	1 Corinthians 10:32
Acts 8:38-39	1 Corinthians 11:2
Acts 9:18	1 Corinthians 12:13
Acts 10:44-48	1 Corinthians 12:12-13
Acts 10:48	1 Corinthians 13:13-15
Acts 11:15-18	1 Corinthians 14:22
Acts 11:17	1 Corinthians 14:26
Acts 11:24	1 Corinthians 14:33
Acts 13:24	1 Corinthians 14:40
Acts 15:14	1 Corinthians 15:29
Acts 16:15	1 Corinthians 15:51
Acts 16:30-31	2 Corinthians 11:15
Acts 16:31	Galatians 2:16
Acts 16:33	Galatians 3:10
Acts 17:10-13	Galatians 3:24
Acts 18:8	Galatians 3:28
Acts 19:1-6	Galatians 4:6
Acts 19:1-7	Ephesians 1:11-12
Acts 19:5	Ephesians 1:12-13
Acts 22:16	Ephesians 2:8-9

Ephesians 2:20
Ephesians 3:5
Ephesians 3:9
Ephesians 3:17-19
Ephesians 4:5
Ephesians 4:4-5
Ephesians 4:5-6
Ephesians 5:18-19
Ephesians 5:25-27
Ephesians 5:26
Ephesians 5:32
Ephesians 6:17
Philippians 3:9
Philippians 4:19
Colossians 1:26-27
Colossians 2:11-12
Colossians 2:11-13

Colossians 2:16-17
Titus 1:5
Titus 3:5
Hebrews 4:12
Hebrews 6:2
James 2:10
1 Peter 1:7
1 Peter 3:20-21
1 Peter 3:21
2 Peter 2:1
2 Peter 3:9
1 John 1:4
1 John 1:8-10
2 John 1:12
Revelation 3:18
Revelation 22:20

INDEX OF WORDS AND PHRASES

APPENDIX A – SCRIPTURES THAT INCLUDE: BAPTIZE(D), BAPTIST, BAPTISM(S) IN THE BIBLE

In those days came John the <u>Baptist</u>, preaching in the wilderness of Judaea, (Matt 3:1)

And were <u>baptized</u> of him in Jordan, confessing their sins. (Matt 3:6)

But when he saw many of the Pharisees and Sadducees come to his <u>baptism</u>, he said unto them, O generation of vipers, who hath warned you to flee from the wrath to come? (Matt 3:7)

I indeed <u>baptize</u> you with water unto repentance: but he that cometh after me is mightier than I, whose shoes I am not worthy to bear: he shall <u>baptize</u> you with the Holy Ghost, and with fire: (Matt 3:11)

Then cometh Jesus from Galilee to Jordan unto John, to be <u>baptized</u> of him. (Matt 3:13)

But John forbad him, saying, I have need to be baptized of thee, and comest thou to me? (Matt 3:14)

And Jesus, when he was <u>baptized</u>, went up straightway out of the water: and, lo, the heavens were opened unto him, and he saw *the Spirit of God descending like a dove, and lighting upon him:* **(Matt 3:16)**

Verily I say unto you, Among them that are born of women there hath not risen a greater than John the <u>Baptist</u>: notwithstanding he that is least in the kingdom of heaven is greater than he. **(Matt 11:11)**

And from the days of John the <u>Baptist</u> until now the kingdom of heaven suffereth violence, and the violent take it by force. **(Matt 11:12)**

And said unto his servants, This is John the <u>Baptist</u>; he is risen from the dead; and therefore mighty works do shew forth themselves in him. **(Matt 14:2)**

And she, being before instructed of her mother, said, Give me here John <u>Baptist's</u> head in a charger. **(Matt 14:8)**

And they said, Some say that thou art John the <u>Baptist</u>: some, Elias; and others, Jeremias, or one of the prophets. **(Matt 16:14)**

Then the disciples understood that he spake unto them of John the <u>Baptist</u>. **(Matt 17:13)**

But Jesus answered and said, Ye know not what ye ask. Are ye able to drink of the cup that I shall drink of, and to be <u>baptized</u> with the *baptism* that I am baptized with? They say unto him, We are able. *(Matt 20:22)*

And he saith unto them, Ye shall drink indeed of my cup, and be *baptized* with the *baptism* that I am *baptized* with: but to sit on my right hand, and on my left, is not mine to give, but it shall be given to them for whom it is prepared of my Father. *(Matt 20:23)*

The *baptism* of John, whence was it? from heaven, or of men? This should be togetherAnd they reasoned with themselves, saying, If we shall say, From heaven; he will say unto us, Why did ye not then believe him? *(Matt 21:25)*

Go ye therefore, and teach all nations, *baptizing* them in the name of the Father, and of the Son, and of the Holy Ghost: *(Matt 28:19)*

John did *baptize* in the wilderness, and preach the *baptism* of repentance for the remission of sins. *(Mark 1:4)*

And there went out unto him all the land of Judaea, and they of Jerusalem, and were all *baptized* of him in the river of Jordan, confessing their sins. *(Mark 1:5)*

I indeed have *baptized* you with water: but he shall *baptize* you with the Holy Ghost. *(Mark 1:8)*

And it came to pass in those days, that Jesus came from Nazareth of Galilee, and was <u>baptized</u> of John in Jordan. **(Mark 1:9)**

And king Herod heard of him; (for his name was spread abroad:) and he said, That John the <u>Baptist</u> was risen from the dead, and therefore mighty works do shew forth themselves in him. **(Mark 6:14)**

And she went forth, and said unto her mother, What shall I ask? And she said, The head of John the <u>Baptist</u>. **(Mark 6:24)**

And she came in straightway with haste unto the king, and asked, saying, I will that thou give me by and by in a charger the head of John the <u>Baptist</u>. **(Mark 6:25)**

And they answered, John the <u>Baptist</u>: but some say, Elias; and others, One of the prophets. **(Mark 8:28)**

But Jesus said unto them, Ye know not what ye ask: can ye drink of the cup that I drink of? and be <u>baptized</u> with the <u>baptism</u> that I am <u>baptized</u> with? **(Mark 10:38)**

And they said unto him, We can. And Jesus said unto them, Ye shall indeed drink of the cup that I drink of; and with the <u>baptism</u> that I am <u>baptized</u> withal shall ye be <u>baptized</u>: **(Mark 10:39)**

The _baptism_ of John, was it from heaven, or of men? answer me. *(Mark 11:30)*

He that believeth and is _baptized_ shall be saved; but he that believeth not shall be damned. *(Mark 16:16)*

And he came into all the country about Jordan, preaching the _baptism_ of repentance for the remission of sins; *(Luke 3:3)*

Then said he to the multitude that came forth to be _baptized_ of him, O generation of vipers, who hath warned you to flee from the wrath to come? *(Luke 3:7)*

Then came also publicans to be _baptized_, and said unto him, Master, what shall we do? *(Luke 3:12)*

John answered, saying unto them all, I indeed _baptize_ you with water; but one mightier than I cometh, the latchet of whose shoes I am not worthy to unloose: he shall _baptize_ you with the Holy Ghost and with fire: *(Luke 3:16)*

Now when all the people were _baptized_, it came to pass, that Jesus also being _baptized_, and praying, the heaven was opened, *(Luke 3:21)*

When the men were come unto him, they said, John _Baptist_ hath sent us unto thee, *saying, Art thou he that should come? or look we for another? (Luke 7:20)*

For I say unto you, Among those that are born of women there is not a greater prophet than John the <u>Baptist</u>: but he that is least in the kingdom of God is greater than he. (Luke 7:28)

And all the people that heard him, and the publicans, justified God, being <u>baptized</u> with the <u>baptism</u> of John. (Luke 7:29)

But the Pharisees and lawyers rejected the counsel of God against themselves, being not <u>baptized</u> of him. (Luke 7:30)

For John the <u>Baptist</u> came neither eating bread nor drinking wine; and ye say, He hath a devil. (Luke 7:33)

They answering said, John the <u>Baptist</u>; but some say, Elias; and others say, that one of the old prophets is risen again. (Luke 9:19)

But I have a <u>baptism</u> to be <u>baptized</u> with; and how am I straitened till it be accomplished! (Luke 12:50)

The <u>baptism</u> of John, was it from heaven, or of men? (Luke 20:4)

And they asked him, and said unto him, Why <u>baptizest</u> thou then, if thou be not that

Christ, nor Elias, neither that prophet? **(John 1:25)**

John answered them, saying, I <u>baptize</u> with water: but there standeth one among you, whom ye know not; **(John 1:26)**

These things were done in Bethabara beyond Jordan, where John was <u>baptizing</u>. **(John 1:28)**

And I knew him not: but that he should be made manifest to Israel, therefore am I come <u>baptizing</u> with water. **(John 1:31)**

And I knew him not: but he that sent me to <u>baptize</u> with water, the same said unto me, Upon whom thou shalt see the Spirit descending, and remaining on him, the same is he which <u>baptizeth</u> with the Holy Ghost. **(John 1:33)**

After these things came Jesus and his disciples into the land of Judaea; and there he tarried with them, and <u>baptized</u>. **(John 3:22)**

And John also was <u>baptizing</u> in Aenon near to Salim, because there was much water there: and they came, and were <u>baptized</u>. **(John 3:23)**

And they came unto John, and said unto him, Rabbi, he that was with thee beyond Jordan, to whom thou barest witness, behold, the same _baptizeth,_ and all men come to him. *(John 3:26)*

When therefore the Lord knew how the Pharisees had heard that Jesus made and _baptized_ more disciples than John, *(John 4:1)*

(Though Jesus himself _baptized_ not, but his disciples,) *(John 4:2)*

And went away again beyond Jordan into the place where John at first _baptized;_ and there he abode. *(John 10:40)*

For John truly baptized with water; but ye shall be baptized with the Holy Ghost not many days hence. *(Acts 1:5)*

Beginning from the _baptism_ of John, unto that same day that he was taken up from us, must one be ordained to be a witness with us of his resurrection. *(Acts 1:22)*

Then Peter said unto them, Repent, and be _baptized_ every one of you in the name of Jesus Christ for the remission of sins, and ye shall receive the gift of the Holy Ghost. *(Acts 2:38)*

Then they that gladly received his word were _baptized:_ and the same day there were added unto them about three thousand souls. *(Acts 2:41)*

But when they believed Philip preaching the things concerning the kingdom of God, and the name of Jesus Christ, they were baptized, both men and women. (Acts 8:12)

Then Simon himself believed also: and when he was baptized, he continued with Philip, and wondered, beholding the miracles and signs which were done. (Acts 8:13)

(For as yet he was fallen upon none of them: only they were baptized in the name of the Lord Jesus.) (Acts 8:16)

And as they went on their way, they came unto a certain water: and the eunuch said, See, here is water; what doth hinder me to be baptized? (Acts 8:36)

And he commanded the chariot to stand still: and they went down both into the water, both Philip and the eunuch; and he baptized him. (Acts 8:38)

And immediately there fell from his eyes as it had been scales: and he received sight forthwith, and arose, and was baptized. (Acts 9:18)

That word, I say, ye know, which was published throughout all Judaea, and began from Galilee, after the baptism which John preached; (Acts 10:37)

Can any man forbid water, that these should not be <u>baptized</u>, which have received the Holy Ghost as well as we? *(Acts 10:47)*

And he commanded them to be <u>baptized</u> in the name of the Lord. Then prayed they him to tarry certain days. *(Acts 10:48)*

Then remembered I the word of the Lord, how that he said, John indeed <u>baptized</u> with water; but ye shall be <u>baptized</u> with the Holy Ghost. *(Acts 11:16)*

When John had first preached before his coming the <u>baptism</u> of repentance to all the people of Israel. *(Acts 13:24)*

And when she was <u>baptized</u>, and her household, she besought us, saying, If ye have judged me to be faithful to the Lord, come into my house, and abide there. And she constrained us. *(Acts 16:15)*

And he took them the same hour of the night, and washed their stripes; and was <u>baptized</u>, he and all his, straightway. *(Acts 16:33)*

And Crispus, the chief ruler of the synagogue, believed on the Lord with all his house; and many of the Corinthians hearing believed, and were <u>baptized</u>. *(Acts 18:8)*

This man was instructed in the way of the Lord; and being fervent in the spirit, he *spake and taught diligently the things of the Lord, knowing only the baptism of John. (Acts 18:25)*

And he said unto them, Unto what then were ye baptized? And they said, Unto John's baptism. (Acts 19:3)

Then said Paul, John verily baptized with the baptism of repentance, saying unto the people, that they should believe on him which should come after him, that is, on Christ Jesus. (Acts 19:4)

When they heard this, they were baptized in the name of the Lord Jesus. (Acts 19:5)

And now why tarriest thou? arise, and be baptized, and wash away thy sins, calling on the name of the Lord. (Acts 22:16)

Know ye not, that so many of us as were baptized into Jesus Christ were baptized into his death? (Rom 6:3)

Therefore we are buried with him by baptism into death: that like as Christ was raised up from the dead by the glory of the Father, even so we also should walk in newness of life. (Rom 6:4)

Is Christ divided? was Paul crucified for you? or were ye baptized in the name of Paul? (1Cor 1:13)

I thank God that I <u>baptized</u> none of you, but Crispus and Gaius; **(1Cor 1:14)**

Lest any should say that I had <u>baptized</u> in mine own name. **(1Cor 1:15)**

And I <u>baptized</u> also the household of Stephanas: besides, I know not whether I baptized any other. **(1Cor 1:16)**

For Christ sent me not to <u>baptize</u>, but to preach the gospel: not with wisdom of words, lest the cross of Christ should be made of none effect. **(1Cor 1:17)**

And were all <u>baptized</u> unto Moses in the cloud and in the sea; **(1Cor 10:2)**

For by one Spirit are we all <u>baptized</u> into one body, whether we be Jews or Gentiles, whether we be bond or free; and have been all made to drink into one Spirit. **(1Cor 12:13)**

Else what shall they do which are <u>baptized</u> for the dead, if the dead rise not at all? why are they then <u>baptized</u> for the dead? **(1Cor 15:29)**

For as many of you as have been <u>baptized</u> into Christ have put on Christ. **(Gal 3:27)**

One Lord, one faith, one <u>baptism</u>, **(Eph 4:5)**

Buried with him in <u>baptism</u>, wherein also ye are risen with him through the faith of the *operation of God, who hath raised him from the dead. (Col 2:12)*

Of the doctrine of <u>baptisms</u>, and of laying on of hands, and of resurrection of the dead, and of eternal judgment. (Heb 6:2)

The like figure whereunto even <u>baptism</u> doth also now save us (not the putting away of the filth of the flesh, but the answer of a good conscience toward God,) by the resurrection of Jesus Christ: (1Pet 3:21)

APPENDIX B – STRONG'S REFERENCES FOR THE DOCTRINE OF BAPTISMS

G907 βαπτίζω **baptizo** (bap-tid'-zo) v.
[from a derivative of G911]   *KJV: Baptist,   baptize,   wash(ed)*
     Root(s): G911

G910 **Βαπτιστής Baptistes** (bap-tis-tace') n/p.
[from G907   *KJV: Baptist*   Root(s): G907

G908 βάπτισμα **baptisma** (bap'-tis-mah) n.
[from G907]   *KJV: baptism*   Root(s): G907

G911 βάπτω **bapto** (bap'-to) v.
[a primary verb]   *KJV: dip*

G909 βαπτισμός **baptismos** (bap-tis-mos') n.
[from G907]   *KJV: baptism, washing*   Root(s): G907

ABOUT THE AUTHOR

By God's grace, Dr. Luis Ruiz has served as a Pastor and a Chaplain for the furtherance of the Gospel of Christ. An evangelist since 2010, he has preached in many churches throughout the United States.

He currently teaches a wide-range of classes in the fields of theology, Biblical studies, management and leadership. He has taught at 5 different universities and a seminary as a Full-Time and an Adjunct Professor.

Writing for both Christian and secular publications, in 2013, Dr. Ruiz published *"Pride's Consequences & Humility's Blessings"*. In 2019, he published a peer-reviewed article in the renowned International Journal of Management & Decision Making.

Outside of teaching and ministry, he has 25 years of domestic & international corporate leadership experience working for several Fortune 100 companies in the fields of sales management, marketing strategy and market analytics. An invited conference speaker, he has travelled professionally throughout North America, South America and Europe.

Luis is married to Delia and both reside with their three wonderful teenage children.

CPSIA information can be obtained
at www.ICGtesting.com
Printed in the USA
BVHW052139260720
584573BV00008BA/93